Spanish History

A Captivating Guide to the History of Spain and the Basques

Free Bonus from Captivating History (Available for a Limited time)

Hi History Lovers!

Now you have a chance to join our exclusive history list so you can get your first history ebook for free as well as discounts and a potential to get more history books for free! Simply visit the link below to join.

Captivatinghistory.com/ebook

Also, make sure to follow us on Facebook, Twitter and Youtube by searching for Captivating History.

Table of Contents

Part 1: History of Spain

A Captivating Guide to Spanish History, Starting from Roman Hispania through the Visigoths, the Spanish Empire, the Bourbons, and the War of Spanish Independence to the Present

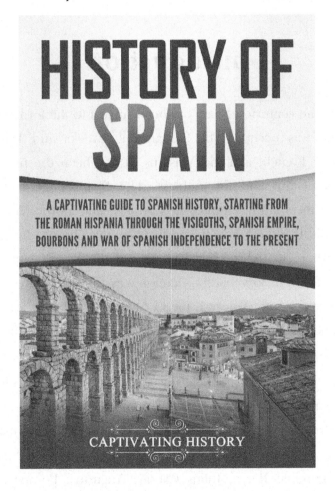

Introduction

Throughout the centuries, Spain has been subject to the lordship of other countries. It was occupied by the ancient Greeks and Romans, the Visigoths, the French, and the Muslims. It has been the playground of both the respectful and the ruthless. The Spanish coasts have been occupied by the trading empires of Carthage and Rome. All that time, Spain was told by others how to run their country, how to fight, whom to fight, and where to fight. They had one of the largest empires in the world—something history barely mentions—as they had acres of land in both North and South America, the Caribbean, Mesoamerica, and some islands in the Mediterranean. Evidence of Spanish architecture dots the world.

Yet Spain was also a battlefield for countries fighting for other causes. They were sucked into wars fought by the Carthaginians, Romans, Moors, Visigoths, British, French, Portuguese, Dutch, and Austrians, just to name a few. Some of the most famous men in history traversed Spanish soil, including Hannibal Barca, Julius Caesar, Augustus, Pompey, Hadrian,

Vespasian, Trajan, Marcus Aurelius, and Napoleon. Four Roman emperors were born there, and Augustus Caesar spent his vacations there. Pablo Picasso was born in Spain, while El Greco moved there.

Many different countries and forces have had control of Spain throughout the years. Not too long ago, Spain was burdened with a dictatorship and suffered through a civil war, yet today it is an independent democracy. But how did its people do that? This book will examine the highs and lows of Spanish history and will hopefully pique your interest in learning more about it.

Chapter 1 – Prehistory

Archaeologists have found skeletal remains of early hominids in the Iberian Peninsula, which is located in the southwestern corner of Europe. These date back to the Pleistocene geological epoch when glaciers were just subsiding from the continents. It is estimated that the Pleistocene period began about thirty million years ago and ended around 11,700 years ago. The glaciers melted below the north latitude of 40°. Due to the glacial melting, sea levels rose. That, in turn, caused temporal land depressions, in which marine fossils have been found.

The earliest appearance of hominids in the Iberian Peninsula occurred during the first period of the Stone Age, that is, the Paleolithic age.

Stone Age

Around 2.5 million years ago, civilization fashioned stone tools for hunting, agriculture, cooking, and the like. Prehistoric mankind shaped these tools by striking an object repeatedly with a harder stone. The problem with stone tools is that they are crude, and it was laborious or impossible to shape them into a more useful shape. The Stone Age ended around 10,000 BCE.

Paleolithic Era

During the Paleolithic Era (the Old Stone Age), there were sub-periods/cultures that can be identified by the various tools used and the cave art. These periods, which tended to overlap, include:

The Châtelperronian

The Gravettian

The Aurignacian

The Solutrean

The Magdalenian

The Azilian

Cave art from the Châtelperronian culture has been found in the El Pendo Cave in the Cantabrian region of Spain (north-central and northeastern Spain) and depict animals they hunted. These people were hunter-gatherers who lived in communities of thirty to forty people.

The Gravettian hunting tools date back to 35,000 years ago. Tools produced during that time were tanged arrowheads, boomerangs, and blunt-backed knives.

The tools used during the Aurignacian period, which followed, include the use of bones, antlers, flint, ivory, and the like. Archaeological evidence from this period was found in the Cantabrian Mountains, which run east/west across northern Spain. The Aurignacian tools were more advanced, consisting of antler points and worked bone. The people also had flint stone tools that had notches along their blades and were more carefully hewn.

Approximately 22,000 years ago, the Solutrean culture was formed. Artifacts from that period were found in some early settlements along the northern coast of the Cantabrian Sea and the Bay of Biscay. The land of the Astures lay just toward the western areas of the Cantabrian Mountains. Many Solutrean artifacts have been found there. To the east lay the Vasco-Cantabrian region, which was peopled with the tribes of the Vascones, the Tarbelli, and the Caristiis.

Tools used during the Magdalenian period were usually small arrowheads, barbs made of flint, and chert, which was made of silica. Azilian tools were made approximately 10,000 to 12,500 years ago. They were cruder and less expensive.

<u>Paleolithic Art</u>

In north-central Spain, many cave paintings were found in the Cave of Altamira. They were done between 35,000 and 11,000 years ago. There are actually eighteen caves there, and the styles manifest the characteristics of the four cultures noted above: Aurignacian, Gravettian, Solutrean, and Magdalenian. Researchers also added another culture that is more specific to the Franco-Cantabrian region: the Azilian. Cave paintings from the Azilian culture have been found across northern Spain and southwestern France.

The cave art was done during the Solutrean and the Magdalenian periods. Only the mouth of the cave shows signs of human habitation, as the paintings themselves are spread throughout the length of the cave. People used charcoal and hematite, an iron ore, to create this art. The pigments were made from those materials by diluting them, and there were efforts to provide the impression of light and shadow.

The more common subjects in the paintings are an extinct species of bison—the steppe bison—horses, deer, and what looks like a wild boar. Bison representations are the most common. Images of goats were also found, along with handprints. The handprints were made by blowing pigment over one's hands to leave a negative image.

Archeologists have dated some of the paintings in the El Pendo Cave in Cantabria back to approximately 33,000 years ago during what was called the Gravettian period. Common themes were of animals that the people hunted, such as ibexes (wild goats), deer, and horses.

The El Pendo Cave was a continual Neanderthal settlement for thousands of years. It has been studied extensively by the Catalan Institute of Human Paleoecology and Social Evolution in Tarragona, Spain, along with the Institute for Prehistoric Research of the University of Cantabria. It was active between 50,000 to 60,000 years ago.

The Cave of la Clotilde in Reocín, Spain, in the Cantabrian region, has artifacts and cave paintings from the Magdalenian period between 17,000 to 12,000 years ago. The tools used then were more refined, and there was evidence the people used carbide, a mixture of carbon and some type of metallic substance. When they fashioned these tools, some of the carbide was preheated beforehand.

The Mesolithic Age

Around 10,000 BCE, the Magdalenian tools developed and began using more geometric shapes, such as triangles, and stone tools became smaller and more portable. Climatologists indicate the area was warming up. Not only were prehistoric tools found in the Cantabrian area, but they were also found farther south around Valencia and near the Mediterranean coast.

Evidence indicates that the people created semi-permanent settlements. Several villages, which held about 600 people, were found along the northern borders of the Cantabrian Sea and the Bay of Biscay. The people hunted herds of bison, wild horses, and reindeer, along with other animals, with traps, spears, nets, and snares.

Toolmaking was a commonly practiced trade. In their humble villages, there were burins (chisels), hammers, borers, wedges, barbed points, and bones that were cut in such a way as to make primitive saws. Their art manifested more naturalism. Jewelry was made, and scenes were actually painted on cave walls. Their drawings were better and showed more perspective, and there were attempts to picture things more realistically.

The Neolithic Age

The Stone Age has been subdivided into smaller segments, and one of the most important is the Neolithic Age, as significant changes occurred during that time. It is also called the New Stone Age, and it started around the 6th millennium BCE. During this time, warmer weather helped the community develop agriculture in addition to hunting to provide for themselves. This period was important because it showed a significant change in the development of civilization, specifically the introduction of agriculture. During that time, the tribes built villages instead of using temporary shelters to follow herds of wild animals.

The people had already started to grow cereal crops and ate olives. It's unknown as to whether or not they raised olive trees or ate the olives from wild trees.

Red pottery called "La Almagra" was discovered in Andalusia in southern Spain from the Neolithic era. It is made of red slip clay and is generally smooth. In several areas in southern Spain, Cardial pottery was developed. This pottery shows decorative elements, such as impressions of shells or lines and curves made with a nail or comb.

Funerary Rites

Burial rites were also established, as archaeologists have discovered dolmens. These are stone monuments consisting of two vertical stones supporting a horizontal stone, marking the sites where loved ones were buried. The remains of humans were found there, but researchers aren't sure if the remains were placed there when the people were buried. At the moment, it is impossible to date the placement of the stones with the time of the burial. Archaeologists have made the assumption that these served as markers for tombs, although there is not enough clear evidence to support this claim.

<u>Astonishing Find!</u>

Just recently, there was an astounding find from the Middle Neolithic period, which lasted between around 4800 to 4200 BCE. According to the Department of Prehistory and Archaeology at the University of Seville, two adult human skulls were found, one male and the other female, along with the skeleton of a young goat, in the Dehesilla Cave in Cádiz, Spain. It was a gravesite, but it was unlike other Neanderthal burial sites.

On the female's skull, there was evidence of a possible decapitation, and on the front of the skull, archaeologists found evidence of trepanation. Trepanation is a surgical technique in which a hole is drilled into the skull. One theory indicates that this may have been an attempt to alleviate a physical malady or was possibly a cure for a mental condition. An archaeological team under the direction of Daniel García-Rivero suggested that this was possibly a funerary ritual in which human sacrifice took a prominent role.

Bronze Age

The Bronze Age came later to Spain than to other countries due to the paucity of the copper needed to create bronze. In the El Argar site in southeastern Spain, bronze artifacts have been dated to around 1750 BCE. Bronze is a mixture of copper and tin. Many areas in Eurasia didn't have natural sources of tin, but the Iberian Peninsula was (and still is) rich with it. Copper, on the other hand, had to be transported from the Middle East or Indian subcontinent. Knives, spears, swords, arrow points, and large axes were all found at El Argar. The difficulties people had with bronze tools was that they broke or bent too easily.

The Tartessian culture rose in southwestern Iberia during the Bronze Age in the late 9th century BCE. Its influence spread to Extremadura in western Iberia.

Iron Age

The Greek seafarers arrived around the 9th century BCE. They used the southern coastal areas of Spain to set up trading ports near the mouth of the Ebro River, which originates in north-central Spain and flows in a southerly direction into the Mediterranean Sea. In fact, the word "Iberia" came from the Greeks. They adapted it from the Latin word "Hiberia," which was derived from the Hiberius River (now known as the Ebro River).

The Iberians were the people who dwelt in the eastern and southern coasts of the Iberian Peninsula. The term "Iberian" was generally used to refer to all the people who lived on the peninsula, regardless of their ethnicity.

In the late 8th century BCE, northeastern Iberia developed metallurgy using iron. Evidence has been found along the lower Ebro River, and it spread as far south as Castellón along the Mediterranean Sea. Greek colonies were created at Empúries along the lower eastern coast of the Mediterranean Sea.

Hominid Remains

A huge archaeological site was found in the Atapuerca Mountains, located in northern Spain, in the 20th century. Since then, its various underground levels have been continually excavated and studied. Most of the artifacts and human bones left there date to the Stone Age, but some of the levels contain artifacts from the Bronze Age.

As one might expect, the archaeological site of Atapuerca, which is today a UNESCO World Heritage Site, contains human remains. One of mankind's earliest ancestors, *Homo heidelbergensis*, was discovered there. *Homo heidelbergensis* shares characteristics of two verified ancestors of mankind: *Homo erectus* and *Homo sapiens*, today's humans. DNA evidence also showed there were bone fragments from *Homo neanderthalensis* (Neanderthals).

Many researchers have said that *Homo heidelbergensis* was a separate species, while others have argued that it evolved into *Homo neanderthalensis*. A distinct population of them evolved into Cro-Magnons and today's humans, *Homo sapiens*.

Skull of Homo heidelbergensis found in Spain

Rept0n1x, CC BY-SA 3.0 <https://creativecommons.org/licenses/by-sa/3.0>, via Wikimedia Commons https://commons.wikimedia.org/wiki/File:Skull,_Natural_History_Museum,_London_-_DSCF0431.JPG

The earliest Iberians were hunter-gatherers. They hunted the great wooly mammoths, saber-toothed cats, and giant sloths. These people were nomadic, as they needed to follow the animal herds.

In Escoural Cave in Montemor-o-Novo, Portugal, evidence of temporary settlements of Neanderthals was uncovered. Neanderthal remains were also found in Forbes' Quarry in Gibraltar; Zafarraya, a province of Granada, Spain; and the Cave of Salemas and the Cave of Pego do Diabo in Loures, Portugal.

The Neanderthals, who were descendants of the Cro-Magnons, gave rise to modern man. The period in which they lived may have overlapped the time when the Neanderthals existed. Evidence of this can be ascertained by the discovery of the "Lapedo child," whose mandible and cranium appear to be a hybrid between a Cro-Magnon and a Neanderthal. However, this claim has been contested, although more recent genetic work shows the possibility of the child being a hybrid.

Early Tribes

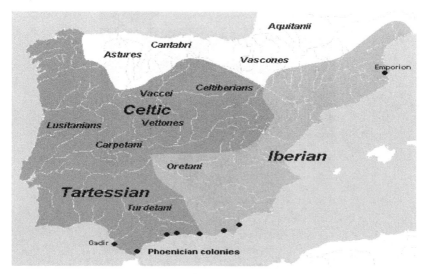

Early tribes of the Iberian Peninsula
https://en.wikipedia.org/wiki/File:Languages_of_pre-Roman_Iberia.gif

Although it is not exactly known when the first humans arrived on the Iberian Peninsula, etymologists have studied language patterns and indicated that the Vascones, Aquitanians, Cantabrians, and Astures arrived during Paleolithic times and predate the arrival of other tribes on the Iberian Peninsula. The ancient historians, such as Titus Livius (Livy), Strabo, Gaius Plinius Secundus (Pliny the Elder), and Claudius

Ptolemaeus (Ptolemy), first recorded them.

The next peoples to arrive came from eastern Eurasia, and they originated from the steppes around the Caspian Sea. They migrated westward and settled in the main area of the Iberian Peninsula. The basic tribal divisions that were noted include the Iberians, the Celts, the Lusitanians, and the Tartessians. Along the southern and eastern coasts, the Carthaginians, Phoenicians, and Greeks established settlements. Those coastal settlements were more like colonies. These civilizations used them for trading purposes, as they were all seafaring people whose homelands were elsewhere.

Chapter 2 – The First and Second Punic Wars

Prelude to War

In 270 BCE, the native people of Messana (Messina) in Sicily were occupied by the Mamertines. Hiero II, the king of the neighboring city of Syracuse on the eastern coast of Sicily, vehemently objected to that. The Mamertines felt threatened and turned to the Carthaginians and the Romans for help. Carthage responded first and established a garrison in Messana.

While the Roman Senate took some time to decide as to whether or not to intervene, Rome saw this as a golden opportunity to gain control of the Mediterranean and expand beyond Italy. As a result, Consul Appius Claudius was ordered to enter and conquer Messana in 264/263 BCE.

The First Punic War (264–241 BCE)

The word "Punic" is derived from the Latin words "poenus" and "punicus." It was intended to refer to the Carthaginians. In the course of its expansion, Carthage needed control over Sicily, an island off the western tip of Italy in the central Mediterranean. They already had established a base at Agrigento (also known as Akragas or Agrigentum) in southern Sicily.

The Battle of Messana

In 264 BCE, the Romans entered Sicily in the east and rapidly defeated Hiero II of Syracuse before going after the Carthaginians at Messana. Both infantries engaged each other, with their cavalries fighting at each end of the flanks. The Romans were disciplined soldiers and expelled the Carthaginians from the city.

Rome looked upon Sicily as a golden opportunity to expand out of Italy and gain control in the Mediterranean. In 263 BCE, Rome persuaded the independent territory of Syracuse on the eastern edge of Sicily to join them in ejecting Carthage from their base at Agrigento.

Battle of Agrigento

In 262 BCE, Carthaginian commander Hanno stationed himself outside the city along with his troops and elephants, which the Carthaginians were fond of using in battles. About twenty-five miles away from them, Roman commanders Lucius Postumius Megellus and Quintus Mamilius Vitulus were stationed with their forces. From his position, Hanno was able to cut off the supply line for the Romans encamped there. Hanno had hoped that the Romans would be defeated by their own hunger, so he waited for the Romans to leave or surrender. Six months passed, and the Roman soldiers were growing weak and ill; many were close to desertion. Hanno continued to wait.

In the meantime, the Carthaginian general Hannibal Gisco, who was inside the city with his troops, was getting desperate after the six-month siege because food for himself and his troops was running low, so he cleverly sent up smoke signals to Hanno for help.

Although there are two versions of what happened during the attack, the most likely one has to do with a cavalry and an elephant attack by Hanno in the beginning, followed by an attack on the tight Roman maniple formations of several split legions. The Romans managed to panic the elephants, which caused pandemonium, and the Romans won the battle. No doubt embarrassed by his failure, Hanno was forced to retreat.

The Romans took possession of the city and enslaved the population. Despite that, Hannibal and some of his forces escaped unharmed.

The campaign then moved to Lilybaeum in 250 BCE. In 249, while the siege of Lilybaeum was still going on, the Romans decided to attack the Carthaginians at Drepana, Sicily. The Romans dispatched a mighty fleet of their warships to surprise them. However, it was dark, and the Romans got lost. They recovered and counterattacked, but the more maneuverable Carthaginian vessels defeated them.

In 247 BCE, Hamilcar Barca, the father of the famous Hannibal, led an exhausted and limited Carthaginian land force. He fought a guerilla-style battle outside of Drepana and managed to hold on to Mount Pellegrino, a small area north of Drepana. Other land battles took place, but they were only on a small scale. Around 241 BCE, when the Carthaginians sent ships into Sicily to supply the forces still there, they were intercepted by an ungraded Roman fleet. The Carthaginians couldn't afford to add to their fleet, and Carthage ordered Hamilcar to seek a peace treaty with Rome.

The Treaty of Lutatius

By virtue of this treaty, which was signed in 241 BCE, Carthage was required to remove any remaining areas they held in Sicily. They had to release all Roman prisoners and pay an indemnity of 3,200 talents of silver.

In 237 BCE, Rome annexed the islands of Sardinia and Corsica from Carthage, while Hamilcar Barca was engaged in a mutinous mercenary rebellion. That was in contravention of the treaty, as Carthage had occupied those islands since the 6th century.

When Carthage attempted to recover the islands of Corsica and Sardinia, Rome considered it an act of war.

The First Punic War was a terrible loss for Carthage, but in a sense, it was a moral loss for Rome. After witnessing the cruelty of the First Punic War, the people of Sicily and other non-Romans were angry and bitter against Rome.

It led the ancient historian Polybius to write, "There is no witness so dreadful, no accuser to terrible, as the conscience that dwells in the heart of every man."

Barcid Spain

After losing their base in Sicily, Hamilcar Barca sought permission from the Carthaginian Senate to recruit a new army. Because the predominant influence in the Senate at the time was Carthage's anti-war faction, which was led by the very conservative Hanno II the Great, there was little objection to maintaining a defensive force.

Once Hamilcar assembled a military force, he deliberately didn't seek any further advice from the pacifist Carthaginian Senate. Instead, he boldly took his forces across the western Mediterranean in 237 BCE. They landed at Gades (Cádiz) on the southwestern coast of the Iberian Peninsula. Hamilcar was anxious to prevent Rome from getting a foothold on all the coastal colonies around the sea. If Carthage had possessions in Iberia, that might help make up for the losses of the First Punic War. The only sea trading colonies that Carthage had in Spain at that time were Gades, Abdera, Malaca, and Sexi.

Hamilcar brought his son-in-law, Hasdrubal the Fair, and his son, Hannibal, along with him. Hamilcar realized that Rome had every intention of subjecting all the nations along the northern Mediterranean, which would cripple Carthage. On one occasion, he took his young son aside and had him make a pledge: "I swear as soon as age will permit, I will use fire and steel to arrest the destiny of Rome."

Next, Hamilcar secured the aid of the Tartessian tribes in order to gain access to the gold and silver mines of Sierra Morena. However, he also needed the cooperation of the Turdetani or Turduli tribe, who dwelled near the foothills of the Sierra Morena. The areas there were occupied by the Celtiberians, and they objected to this intrusion. Hamilcar and his mercenary forces attacked the tribe. Hamilcar won the battle and crucified the Celtiberian commander, but he let 10,000 of the others return home.

Once Hamilcar had control over the mines, he could pay for Iberian mercenaries, which would allow him to secure more control over Iberia. Hamilcar also secured access to the Guadalquiver and Guadalete Rivers in order to set up a mining operation. Once he streamlined the process, Hamilcar was able to send silver back to Carthage to pay off the war debts.

In 236 BCE, he sent Hasdrubal back to North Africa to conduct some campaigns for Carthage. While there, he amassed mercenary soldiers from Numidia and other African regions to take back to Iberia.

In the meantime, Hamilcar traveled eastward toward Cape Nao on the northeastern coast of Iberia and was met with resistance from some Iberian tribes, as well as a smaller tribe, the Bastetani, but overcame them. In 235 BCE, he founded a settlement called Akra Leuke, meaning

"White Mountain." Today, it is known as Alicante. He used Akra Leuke to guard the Carthaginian holdings in southern Iberia.

When Rome heard that Hamilcar was in Iberia, they sent him an inquiry as to his motivations. Fortunately, Hamilcar was able to elude their attention by simply responding that he was raising money to pay off Carthage's war debts.

On his way through Iberia, Hamilcar waged war with the troublesome Oretani tribe. There are multiple theories about the subsequent occurrences. One theory indicates that during the ensuing conflict, the Oretanis sent burning ox carts toward his position. Once the fiery carts crossed the Jucar River, the oxen panicked. Hamilcar was caught up in the melee and died in the chaos. In another version, which was related by the ancient historian Appian, Hamilcar fell from his horse and drowned.

The recorded date for Hamilcar's death was 228 BCE. Carthage had lost one of its most powerful leaders.

The Ebro Treaty

Rome was concerned about Carthage's continued presence in Iberia. Therefore, in 226 BCE, Hamilcar Barca's son-in-law, Hasdrubal the Fair, signed a treaty with Rome, which stated that neither nation would cross the Ebro River. This river runs from northern Spain and into the western Mediterranean Sea. However, this treaty wouldn't last long for too long, as Hannibal was about to enter the picture in a big way.

<u>Battle of Saguntum</u>

In 220 BCE, the city of Saguntum, a Roman ally, was engaged in a civil war. Rome intervened and brought peace to the city. The Roman leaders then advised the city leaders to execute anyone there who supported Carthage's presence on the Iberian Peninsula. The city leaders did so. However, they also, on occasion, attacked neighboring tribes who had good relations with Carthage. Hannibal wanted revenge for that, but he

also wanted to prevent Rome from extending its interests to the rest of Iberia. He mainly wanted to prevent Rome from gaining more control over the Mediterranean Sea trade. Hannibal sought the permission of the Carthaginian Senate to annex Saguntum (today's Sagunto). In addition, Saguntum lay south of the Ebro River, so traveling there wouldn't be a violation of the Ebro Treaty.

Historians estimate that Hannibal set out with 20,000 to 40,000 troops and 40 elephants into southern Iberia. It was said that he financed part of his planned journey with silver from the mines just outside the Carthaginian city of Qart Hadasht (which would later become New Carthage). In 219 BCE, Hannibal Barca captured and secured control of Saguntum on the southern coast of Iberia. Rome demanded that Carthage hand over Hannibal to them and withdraw from Saguntum. Carthage refused, kicking off the Second Punic War.

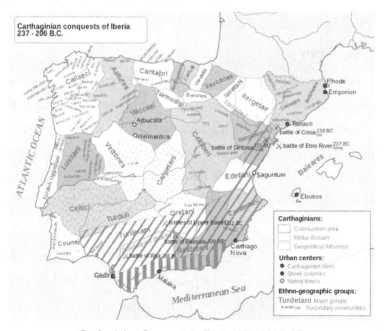

Carthaginian Conquests in Iberia, 237–206 BCE

Alcides Pinto, GFDL <http://www.gnu.org/copyleft/fdl.html>, via Wikimedia Commons
https://commons.wikimedia.org/wiki/File:Iberia_237-206BC.svg

Historians' Argument: Then and Now

Both ancient and contemporary historians have argued about whether or not Hannibal had broken the Ebro Treaty by going north of the Ebro River. Although the map shows that this was clearly not the case, ancient writers like Appian blamed Hannibal for triggering the Second Punic War by crossing the river. Other ancient historians, like Polybius, posed other reasons, but he also mistakenly added that Hannibal had broken the Ebro Treaty, which was untrue.

Many historians—both ancient and contemporary—added to the confusion. For example, Livy, who was known to editorialize, indicated that Hannibal actually said, "It was I who first began that war [the Second Punic War] against the Roman people."

However, it was Rome who crossed the Ebro River when they intervened in Saguntum when it was engaged in a civil war. No doubt, Hannibal also remembered the pledge he had made to his father, the one where he would "arrest the destiny of Rome."

The Second Punic War (218-201 BCE)

The Second Punic War was fought on several fronts, including Iberia, Italy, and North Africa. It was also called the "War against Hannibal," that bold and notorious Carthaginian commander and son of Hamilcar Barca.

Tribal Regions during the Punic Wars

Obsessed with keeping his pledge to his father by destroying Rome, Hannibal boldly marched his troops and elephants through Iberia and Gaul (France) and then over the massive Alps. Men and animals fell just trying to negotiate the treacherous mountain passes in the severe cold of the craggy heights. According to Polybius, 20,000 men perished and most of his elephants. This left about 26,000 men left to fight.

Hannibal spent much of his time in Italy after this point, so his story in Spain ends here. However, the Punic Wars continued to be fought on Spanish soil. Hasdrubal Barca, the younger brother of the famous Hannibal, was in charge of protecting Carthaginian interests along the Ebro River while Hannibal marched toward Italy.

Carthaginian Campaign in Iberia

The Battle of Cissa

In the fall of 218 BCE, the Roman general Gnaeus Cornelius Scipio Calvus landed on the southern Iberian coast at Emporiae (Empúries). The Carthaginian commander Hanno and his Iberian mercenary forces then marched toward the town of Cissa, located on the southeastern coast of Iberia. He had a force of about 11,000 men. The Romans, on the other hand, had twice that number. At the Battle of Cissa, Hanno was captured and lost 8,000 men, with 2,000 of them being taken as prisoners. In addition, Indibilis, the chieftain of the Ilergetes, a small Iberian tribe, was captured along with some of the tribal members. The Romans raided Cissa but were disappointed, as there were little valuables to loot.

The Battle of the Ebro River

In the spring of 217 BCE, Gnaeus Scipio mobilized the Roman navy, taking fifty-five ships to the mouth of the Ebro River in southern Iberia. Hasdrubal Barca ordered Himilco, a Carthaginian leader, to ready their fleet. When the word came, though, Himilco's men had been ashore foraging. Although they rushed back, it was too late. As soon as the

Carthaginian ships exited the mouth of the river, the awaiting Romans sunk four of their vessels and captured two more. Many of the Carthaginians beached their ships and fled. The Romans then towed away twenty-five of the Carthaginians' abandoned ships. The Battle of the Ebro River was a horrendous loss for Carthage.

The Battle of Dertosa

In the spring of 215 BCE, Hasdrubal Barca led the Carthaginian army into the Battle of Dertosa (also known as the Battle of Ibera), in present-day Tortosa, Spain. Hasdrubal went up against two powerful generals, Gnaeus Scipio and his brother Publius Cornelius Scipio. Although the sizes of their forces are unknown, they are estimated to have been around 25,000 each.

Hasdrubal put his unarmored Iberian infantry in the center of the battlefield and his heavily armored troops on the left. His Numidian light cavalry was at the right side of the flank, and his heavier Iberian and Libyan cavalry were on the left. A skirmish line was in front with his elephants.

The Romans used their traditional formation of two legions in the center with Italian forces to either side. Their skirmish line was out front, and its men were armed with javelins.

The Carthaginian cavalry attacked the Romans' flanks, but it still had to do battle with the legions, which rushed forth at them. The Iberians fled from the oncoming onslaught. The Romans then circled around the rear of the Carthaginians, who were now basically surrounded. Hasdrubal and most of the cavalry were able to flee, along with the elephants. The Romans nearly annihilated the Carthaginians who were left behind on the battlefield. It was a disaster for the Carthaginians.

The Battle of the Upper Baetis

This area was the scene of a double battle, that of Castulo and Ilorca. In 212 BCE, Publius and Gnaeus Scipio hired 20,000 Celtiberians to supplement their Roman forces, which had been reduced in the battles with the Carthaginians. Hasdrubal Barca and his brother Mago, along with Hasdrubal Gisco, divided the Carthaginian army into two divisions, which included some allied Iberian forces as well. Publius Scipio attacked Mago at Castulo in south-central Iberia, and Gnaeus Scipio clashed with Hasdrubal Barca at Ilorca to the west.

The Battle of Castulo

Mago Barca and Hasdrubal Gisco held back, instead sending in the Numidian cavalry to harass the Roman troops of Publius Scipio. Publius and his troops dealt with the Numidians and then went after Mago's Iberian allies, who were about to encircle his army. However, the Romans were weakened because they had lost a lot of men to the Numidians. When Hasdrubal Gisco and Mago arrived on the scene, there wasn't much the Romans could do. Many fell on the battlefield that day, including Publius Scipio. It was an incredible victory for the Carthaginians.

The Battle of Ilorca

Prior to the major attack, Hasdrubal Barca and his men had convinced many of Rome's mercenaries not to fight, and they deserted the field. When Gnaeus Scipio was preparing for the attack at Ilorca, he saw the Carthaginian forces racing toward him, which included not just Hasdrubal Barca but also Hasdrubal Gisco and Mago. Because he had already lost many of his warriors to desertion, Gnaeus Scipio tried to withdraw to the north. He was forced to flee to a hilltop, where he tried to dig in. However, the ground was too rocky for digging defensive walls, so they set up their saddles and baggage as a defensive shield. The Carthaginians routed them with ease. Gnaeus Scipio was killed, along with many Roman soldiers as well.

The surviving Romans then headed north of the Ebro River. There were only around 9,000 at that time, which was less than half of their initial number.

The Carthaginians were pleased with their victories at Ilorca and Castulo, and they let the remnants of the Roman army go. That was a dangerous mistake.

Roman Reinforcements Coming!

The year was now 211 BCE. The Carthaginians were benefiting from having conquered nearly half of the Iberian Peninsula. However, some of the Roman survivors who had escaped from the Battles of Castulo and Ilorca contacted Gaius Claudius Nero, the chief Roman general (not to be confused with the emperor of the same name). After the survivors told Nero about their losses in Iberia, he dispatched 13,000 more Roman soldiers to the peninsula. Nero put them under the command of Publius Scipio's son, the more famous Publius (Publius Cornelius Scipio Africanus).

The Romans readied themselves for an attack on the capital of Barcid Spain: Qart Hadasht.

The Siege and Fall of New Carthage

In 209 BCE, Carthage's main seaport of Qart Hadasht, of which they were so proud, was blockaded by a Roman fleet of thirty-five warships. The city was surrounded on three sides by water, so the Carthaginians were basically blocked in. When the Romans arrived, led by Gaius Laelius and Publius Scipio Africanus, the Carthaginian army was ten days away, so the citizen militia had to fend for itself until help arrived. Rome particularly wanted to cut off the financing of Hannibal's march through Italy, as he was getting the silver he needed to pay his soldiers and supplies from Qart Hadasht. Two thousand men slipped out of the city gate to hold off the Romans in their camp to the east and prevent them from using their siege engines to mount the city walls. The Carthaginians were very skilled and fought hard and long against the Roman soldiers. But Scipio had been anticipating such a move, and he forced the Carthaginians to flee back to the city.

Laelius's fleet sailed to the southern side, but the Carthaginians beat them back. Scipio pulled back, but he renewed the assault later in the day. Unfortunately for the Carthaginians, a squall blew through the area, nearly emptying the lagoon to the north. Aided by this twist of fate, the Roman soldiers under Scipio waded through the lagoon, mounted the north wall, and entered the city with ease. The Romans had been ordered to kill everyone they met. Polybius summed up the scene by saying, "One can see...not only humans who have been slaughtered, but even dogs sliced in two and the limbs of other animals cut off."

After taking control of Qart Hadasht, Scipio changed the name of the city to Carthago Nova ("New Carthage").

The Battle of Baecula

In 208 BCE, the Roman commanders had been ordered to stop Hasdrubal Barca, who was on his way through southern Iberia to join his brother, Hannibal, in Italy. At the time, the Carthaginians had about 30,000 men. The Roman commanders, Scipio Africanus and Gaius Laelius, had 30,000 Roman warriors and 10,000 mercenaries.

Hasdrubal spotted the Roman troops and moved to a double-tiered plateau south of the town of Baecula in south-central Iberia. He posted his light troops on the lower level with his main entrenchment behind. There was a valley there, and Scipio dispatched a Roman unit to block the entrance to it so the Carthaginians wouldn't be able to retreat. He also hid his main unit to deceive the Carthaginians. The Romans sent up a volley of arrows and rocks and moved upward toward the Carthaginians. Once the Romans in the front had mounted the incline, Hasdrubal Barca sent out his light troops to attack. Despite their disadvantage, Scipio and his men were able to repel them with ease.

Following that, Gaius Laelius led the heavy Roman forces forward to the right of the enemy, while Scipio hit the left flank. Since Hasdrubal couldn't see the hidden Roman forces, he didn't believe he was dealing with a major conflict, so he didn't properly deploy his men. Once the forces were engaged in hand-to-hand combat, Scipio's hidden unit sprang out and hit Hasdrubal's men. The Romans then slashed at the Carthaginians from three sides.

Once Hasdrubal realized he'd been trapped, he found a way to break through, and he retreated in secret with a smaller force. Even though he tried, Scipio failed to stop his Roman legions from raiding the Carthaginian camp, which delayed him from pursuing Hasdrubal.

The Battle of Ilipa

Hasdrubal Barca had departed Iberia to join up with his brother, Hannibal, in Italy, but he was killed at the Battle of the Metaurus in 207 BCE. Mago Barca and his co-commander, Hasdrubal Gisco, then recruited Celtiberian mercenaries from the central regions of the peninsula. In the spring of 206 BCE, they marched eastward. They had around 54,000 to 74,000 troops and 32 elephants.

Scipio Africanus had approximately 48,000 to 55,000 men, and he sent his troops faster than the Carthaginians. His light troops and cavalry attacked the edges of the Carthaginian flanks. He also attacked the Carthaginian wings, which made it difficult for the Carthaginians to form another sensible defensive formation. Once the Romans had obliterated the Carthaginian forces at the wings, the Carthaginian forces in the center were thrown into confusion when the maddened elephants rushed forward. In the chaos, many Iberian mercenaries deserted.

The Carthaginians, hungry and weary, tried to retreat to their camp. Although they made it back, Scipio ordered a full-scale assault. The remnants that were left fled up a mountain, with the Romans at their heels. When the Romans caught up with them, the butchery commenced.

Mago Barca managed to slip away in the bedlam and headed east along the southern coast of Iberia. He then detoured toward the Balearic Islands in the Mediterranean, where he planned to cross into Italy to help Hannibal. Hasdrubal Gisco left for his home in Carthage. But because he had been unsuccessful, Hasdrubal Gisco was attacked by a mob of angry Carthaginians in 202, and he committed suicide in order to escape their wrath. Livy described him as "the best and most distinguished general this war produced after the three sons of Hamilcar." The Roman consul at the time, Quintus Fabius Maximus Verrucosus, however, insulted his memory by saying that Gisco "showed his speed chiefly in retreat."

After the Battle of Ilipa, about 48,500 Carthaginians had been either killed or captured. Although this wasn't the end of the Second Punic War, it was the end of the conflict in Spain, as the Carthaginians were ejected from Iberia.

Chapter 3 – Rome Entrenching

After the Second Punic War, Publius Scipio Africanus returned from Rome's successful campaign in Africa. He made allies of the various Iberian tribes, agreeing to offer them protection. Ever conscious about defense, the Romans set up permanent garrisons at the key cities of Tarraco (Tarragona) on the southern shore, Carthago Nova (Cartagena) in southeastern Spain, and Gades (Cádiz) on the southwest coast. Scipio insisted that the tribes who had fought against them as mercenaries for Carthage pay tribute, which consisted of clothing, supplies, and food for Roman soldiers who were stationed there. Sardinia and Sicily, which had been ceded to Rome after the Second Punic War, were required to provide the Romans with grain. There were fertile valleys along the Ebro River, and the farmers there produced vegetables for the Romans.

In 218 BCE, Iberia was divided into two provinces: Hispania Citerior ("Nearer Iberia") and Hispania Ulterior ("Further Iberia"). They were named due to their distance from Rome; Hispania Citerior was closer to Rome, while Hispania Ulterior was farther away. Over time, more provinces would be added, which included Hispania Lusitania, no doubt after the tribe who inhabited it, the Lusitanians; Hispania Baetica, which was named after the Bastetani people who inhabited parts of that region there; and Hispania Tarraconensis, after the town of Tarraco in northeastern Hispania.

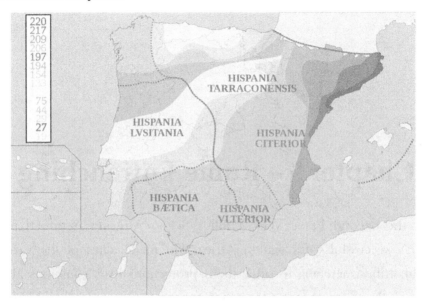

Provinces of Rome by 14 BCE

In 206 BCE, two men, Lucius Cornelius Lentulus and Lucius Manlius Acidinus, were sent to Hispania with powers similar to governors, although they didn't hold the official power of a Roman praetor, which was customary. A praetor was a magistrate who held nearly as much power as a Roman consul, which was the highest office in Rome. The men that were called upon to act as praetors were inexperienced but greedy. They often abused the people and took advantage of their distance from the Roman Senate. In the year 199 BCE, Lentulus and Acidinus were replaced by Gnaeus Cornelius Blasio and Lucius Titus Stertinius; this time around, the two men were praetors.

Things were not always peaceful while Rome established its control. Each province was supported by Roman infantry and cavalry, who were kept occupied by regional wars. In 198 BCE, two Lusitanian chieftains rebelled: Luxinius and Culchas. Just two years later, Hispanic tribes under Budares and Baesadines revolted, and as many as 12,000 Hispanics were slaughtered in the ensuing conflict.

Cato's Campaign

In 197 BCE, Cato became the praetor of Hispania Citerior, and he ruled with an iron fist. One of his sayings was, "War feeds upon itself." Cato used that as a rationale for passing harsh penalties when they were called for. Although he claimed he "pacified Hispania," his actions induced more rebellions. Thus, his own saying, that war feeds upon itself, came true.

Marcus Porcius Cato, who later became a Roman senator, was a military man. He was a strict and exacting leader, and he was sent to Hispania in 195 BCE to calm the rebellions.

Cato the Elder
https://commons.wikimedia.org/wiki/File:Patrizio_Torlonia.jpg

Cato disembarked with his troops at the town of Emporiae, on the border of Hispania and Gaul. He was fierce in his battles, and he was also skilled at bribery and exploitation. Sometimes when fighting broke out in Hispania, he offered to pay the Celtiberians to help him with his campaign. According to ancient biographer Plutarch, when Cato's officers complained that he was paying the "barbarians," he said, "There was nothing terrible in it; should they be victorious, they could pay the price with the spoils taken from the enemy, not out of their own purse." He went on to explain that there would be no record of this payment since it wasn't taken from the Roman treasury.

Cato was a hard-working man who shared his food with his soldiers and worked alongside them. However, he was very much in charge. He planned everything very carefully and coordinated his activities with others. But though he was practical and realistic, he was not a man of compassion. His life was a celebration of the cult of self-aggrandizement.

When Cato became concerned that the tribes north of the Ebro River were becoming restless, he disarmed them all. The Bergistani tribe complained about this, and he leveled the walls of their cities. Once he saw Cato in action, Publius Manilus asked for his help in dealing with the battle preparations of the Turdetani mercenaries. Cato presented them with three options: 1) to return to their homes, 2) to receive double their pay from the Romans, or 3) to set a date for battle. When the mercenaries didn't respond, Cato plundered their lands.

When trouble broke out among other tribes in the Ebro River Basin, Cato captured several towns as a demonstration of his power. After that, the Ausetani, Sedetani, and Suessetani tribes swore their allegiance to him. When a neighboring tribe, the Lancetani, failed to do the same, Cato attacked and subdued them. Whenever a tribe didn't follow his orders, there was always retribution.

The First Celtiberian War (181-179 BCE)

There were six tribal nations who were identified as Celtiberians due to the similarity of their language and appearance. They lived in Hispania Ulterior and Citerior. The tribes were called the Belli, the Arevaci, the Lusones, the Titti, the Vaccaei, and the Pellendones. Praetors Quintus Fulvius Flaccus and Publius Manlius were in charge, and the territory over which they ruled was extended to include some of the neighboring regions for the sake of bringing peace to Iberia.

In 181 BCE, the Celtiberians rebelled against Roman rule. They gathered up an army of 35,000 men and positioned themselves in the central area of Carpetania in the southern regions of Iberia. Flaccus drew up 6,000 infantrymen, who were allies from friendly tribes, along with 3,000 regular Roman soldiers and 300 cavalrymen. Flaccus had his brother, Marcus Fulvius, collect two squads of soldiers and encamp nearby. With his combined army, he defeated the Celtiberians and occupied their town of Aebura.

The Celtiberian forces then moved to Contrebia. However, when they arrived, they saw that the Romans had already occupied it, but the Celtiberians believed they had moved on, so they took no precautions. The Romans suddenly emerged from the city gates and surprised the Celtiberians. The two armies clashed, and as many as 12,000 tribal members were slaughtered. Afterward, the Romans ravaged the countryside.

In 180 BCE, the Romans were reorganizing, and Flaccus was headed for Tarragona on the southeastern coast. The Celtiberians set a trap for him at the Manlian Pass in the mountains. Once Flaccus and his soldiers entered the pass, the Celtiberians leaped upon them from two sides. The Romans drew up their usual tight formation, and the enemy went into a wedge formation to jam them in. With their tight formation, the Romans were able to throw the tribal warriors into disarray. It was a heavy loss for the Celtiberians, who lost 17,000 men.

To aid in the war effort, commanders Tiberius Gracchus and Lucius Postumius Albinus were in charge of maintaining order in Hispania Citerior, and they activated their forces on their side of the border in 179 BCE. Albinus went to the land of the Vaccaei, farther north and east of Celtiberia. Albinus reported that he conquered and killed 35,000 of them.

Gracchus went to the town of Munda and defeated them in a night attack. He took hostages and left a garrison of soldiers behind. While moving on to the town of Certima, he burned the countryside. There, Gracchus was met with messengers from the town, who asked how Gracchus planned on conquering them. Gracchus then showed the envoys the size of his forces. When they saw the size and strength of the Roman forces, the townspeople surrendered without a fight. They were required to pay an indemnity and gave the Romans some of their young nobles to fight alongside them after taking an oath of loyalty to Rome.

Gracchus then moved on to Alce. Here, he planned a feint attack. He sent out his native mercenaries, who pretended to be overwhelmed by the Alce fighters. After seeing that, the Alce soldiers were filled with overconfidence and fiercely attacked. Suddenly, Romans leaped out from behind the ramparts and routed the Alce men, killing 9,000 and taking 320 as prisoners.

In a plundering rampage, Gracchus and his men forced the Celtiberians of 103 towns to submit. Filled with revenge, he returned to Alce and besieged the city. They initially resisted, but when Gracchus employed his siege engines, the people retreated to their citadel and then sent out messengers to offer their surrender. Gracchus accepted the daughter and two sons of the city's powerful chieftain, Thurru, as hostages. Following that, Thurru himself approached Gracchus and asked that his family be spared. Gracchus agreed, and from that point on, Thurru served as a Roman mercenary.

The Second Celtiberian War (154–151 BCE)

By the time the Second Celtiberian War broke out, the Celtiberians had formed a confederacy among their various subtribes, including the Pellendones, the Lusones, the Titti, the Belli, and the Arevaci. Rome was annoyed that the Belli had started building walls around its city of Segeda, and Rome declared war. The Romans intensely disliked any show of resistance, as they felt they were far more superior and needed to keep the tribes subservient.

<u>An Argument about a Wall!</u>

Around 153 BCE, the Belli indicated that they had agreed to the terms laid down by Gracchus and that he hadn't forbidden the construction of a wall around their city of Segeda. The headstrong senators back in Rome disagreed about the construction of the wall and were insulted that they hadn't given special permission for this. The Romans also didn't trust that the Belli would remain peaceful.

The Titti, the Belli, and the Arevaci agreed to participate in the war until arrangements for a peaceful co-existence could be made. However, his rambunctious co-commander, Quintus Fulvius Nobilior, preferred a total and complete surrender.

After seeing these developments, the Belli sought refuge among the Arevaci. The Arevaci even tried to mediate with Nobilior, but it was fruitless. Thus, a courageous Segedan townsman by the name of Carus volunteered to fight. He took 20,000 men and battled with Nobilior and his troops. Nobilior was defeated, but he scored a major victory—the courageous Carus was dead. There were roughly six thousand dead on both sides.

The Arevaci next went to the town of Numantia, where they chose Leuco and Ambo as their leaders. Nobilior raced over there with some Numidian mercenaries and elephants. When the combined Celtiberian forces spotted the huge elephants, they panicked, as they'd never seen elephants before. Thus, the Celtiberians rushed back behind their city walls. A fierce and bloody battle ensued. When a stone hit an elephant squarely on his head, the poor animal went berserk, causing the other elephants to do so as well. As a result, they trampled the Romans!

Marcus Claudius Marcellus replaced Nobilior in 152 BCE. The Arevaci, Titti, and Belli sued for peace. The Roman Senate refused, though, and started gathering troops to send to Hispania. They also appointed Lucius Licinius Lucullus as the new Roman consul in 151 BCE and sent him to replace Marcellus once his term expired. Before that happened, Marcellus really wanted to create a peace arrangement with the tribes. He made a deal through the intercession of Litenno, the Numantine leader. The tribes then handed over the required hostages and sent money to guarantee their promise.

Lucullus's Illegal War

The ambitious Lucullus soon arrived. Instead of leaving matters as they were, he was anxious for fame and stirred up the people, first demonstrating his prowess by attacking the Vaccaei, a peaceful tribe.

He then provoked the Caucaei. When they asked for terms of peace, Lucullus took tribute and had his men kill the adult males in their town of Cauca (today's Coca). Only a few of the inhabitants escaped alive. When reproached for this by the people of Itercatia, Lucullus became furious and laid waste their fields.

Lucullus then went to Pallantia and sent his men out to forage for food. The locals harassed the Romans, making it impossible for Lucullus to get supplies, including the gold and silver he had heard these people possessed. Lucullus was constantly pursued by the Pallantians and other Celtiberians. They chased him and his men north to the Douro River and out of their territory.

The Lusitanians: Terrors of Rome!

When the Carthaginians controlled Hispania, they didn't occupy the whole Iberian Peninsula. However, the arrival of the Romans was a shock for many Hispanic tribes. One such tribe was the Lusitanians in western Hispania.

The Lusitanian War started during the Second Celtiberian War in 155 BCE. It was triggered when Punicus, the chief of the Lusitanians, attacked some of the lands nearby that belonged to Roman subjects. With this move, Punicus gained the support of the Vettones and the Blastophoenicians. However, Punicus was soon killed in a raid. He was succeeded by Caesarus, who continued to rebel against the Roman occupiers. The Treaty of Atilius was signed in 152 BCE, but war erupted again when Lucius Licinius Lucullus, who had fought in the Second Celtiberian War, provoked the Lusitanians.

In 150 BCE, the Roman praetor of the region, Servius Galba, pretended to pacify them, giving them each plots of land on which to farm. In exchange, he promised peace and told them to lay down their arms.

Appian reported that he "told them as friends to lay down their arms." However, when they did so, "he surrounded them with a ditch and sent in soldiers with swords who slew them all. Thus he avenged treachery with treachery in a manner unworthy of a Roman, but imitating barbarians."

Viriathus, the scourge of Rome

Eduardo Barrón, CC BY-SA 3.0 <https://creativecommons.org/licenses/by-sa/3.0>, via Wikimedia Commons https://commons.wikimedia.org/wiki/File:Viriato.JPG

In 148 BCE, the Lusitanians ambushed the Roman soldiers at Tribola. The Lusitanians lost the battle, but a hardy warrior named Viriathus escaped. The Romans received reinforcements, but they, too, were all slain by Viriathus and his men.

In 142 BCE, Fabius Maximus Servilianus then took charge of the Roman legions and marched against Viriathus. Maximus had a tremendous force of 18,000 infantry and 1,600 cavalrymen. Viriathus wasn't able to defeat Maximus, but he and his men were able to inflict 3,000 casualties, but he had to constantly defend himself until the Romans moved on to Itucca. Maximus recaptured some of the cities Viriathus had occupied. It was said that Maximus captured as many as 10,000 men and beheaded 500 of them. The rest were sold into slavery.

In the town of Erisana, Viriathus asked for a peace treaty. The treaty was broken by Rome upon the arrival of Maximus's replacement: Fabius Maximus Caepius. Caepius took over Viriathus's annexed town of Arsa, but Viriathus cleverly escaped. To retaliate, Caepius attacked the neighboring Vettones and Callaici, destroying their crops.

Viriathus still wanted peace, so, in 140 BCE, he sent envoys to the new consul, Quintus Servilius Caepio, to draw up terms. Caepio, though, bribed Viriathus's envoys and had them assassinate Viriathus.

The assassination of Viriathus
https://commons.wikimedia.org/wiki/File:Madrazo_Viriatus_HighRes.jpg

Tautalus replaced Viriathus as the chief of the tribe. He lacked the tactical skills that Viriathus had, and he knew it. Nevertheless, he knew his people counted on him to be honorable and pick up the gauntlet from his illustrious predecessor.

Tautalus took Viriathus's remaining loyal forces and attacked the Roman allies at Saguntum, where he was defeated. From there, he and his men marched to Hispania Ulterior and was confronted with the formidable Roman legions of Caepio at the Baetis River. Tautalus was defeated and surrendered. Caepio gave them lands in southern Iberia, possibly around the city of Valencia.

The Numantine War

The Numantines were a subdivision of the Lusitanians who lived by the Douro River. The Numantines defeated two great Roman generals:

Consul Quintus Caecilius Metellus Macedonicus and Quintus Pompeius. Pompeius, it seems, was a very ineffective Roman soldier. He lost a number of battles to the Numantines, so to avoid future hostilities with the tribe, he negotiated a secret treaty with them. However, the treaty never truly came to fruition, as Marcus Pompillius Laenas soon came to assist in the war effort. When the Numantines returned to complete their obligations under the treaty, Pompeius denied that any treaty existed at all. They sent in Gaius Hostilius Mancinus to subjugate the Numantines. The tough Numantines assaulted Mancinus, and they defeated him until he was forced to accept a treaty. Rome wasn't satisfied and handed over Mancinus to the Numantines to be their prisoner.

In 134 BCE, Rome sent in Consul Scipio Aemilianus to resolve the issue to their liking. He brought a huge army with him, which consisted of 20,000 men and 40,000 allies. Once he arrived at Numantia, he built a ring of seven fortresses around the city. After that, he created a dam out of a nearby swamp, and a lake formed. He had his archers mounted on towers ten feet off the ground, allowing them to easily besiege the city with volley after volley of arrows. Scipio also lowered the Douro River and strung sharp blades across it to prevent anyone from escaping. The Numantines were effectively trapped.

Their leader, Rhetogenes, managed to get out despite the blockade and went to a neighboring region, Lutia, begging for help. The young men from Lutia responded positively, but the more wary Lutian leaders told Scipio about it. In retaliation, Scipio went after the youths and cut off their hands! Such was the cruelty rendered to the people in Iberia.

Numantia sent out ambassadors, offering complete surrender in exchange for freedom. Scipio adamantly refused. He wanted vengeance. When the Numantian envoys returned with the bad news, the incredulous people murdered them for their failure and vehemently refused to surrender.

It was truly the most tragic of tales. When the people started starving, they engaged in cannibalism. Others committed suicide. Eventually, the Romans set fire to the city to force them out. The ancient historian Appian related that, when those who still lived emerged, they came out "looking altogether inhuman, with their bodies unwashed, full of hair and nails and filth; they smelt horribly and their clothing was unwashed and just as stinking...they looked at the Romans in a way which expressed their pride and grief." That tragic year was 133 BCE.

Ruins from the siege of Numantia

Javier Mediavilla Ezquibela, CC BY-SA 3.0 <http://creativecommons.org/licenses/by-sa/3.0/>, via Wikimedia Commons https://commons.wikimedia.org/wiki/File:Esquina_en_Numancia.jpg

Rome Turns Its Attention Elsewhere

Rome tasked the praetors with securing and maintaining peace in the Hispanic provinces. Although the main rebellions—those of the Celtiberians, Lusitanians, and Numantines—were over, the revolts hadn't ended, but they were more sporadic and local. Many may have been resurgences of tribal hostilities that existed prior to the Roman conquest, and others were caused by the restrictions mandated upon the people.

Rome was in the process of building an empire in Western Europe, as well as in Hispania. The Cimbric War, which was fought from 113 to 101

BCE, took place mostly in central Europe, but some of it spilled over into northern Hispania when a Germanic tribe, the Teutons, invaded there. The Celtiberians also involved themselves in the war by crossing the Hispanic borders and fighting against the Teutons and other Germanic tribes.

As for the people of Hispania, the ancient biographer and historian Plutarch commented upon what he saw in the state of Hispania Ulterior. "The province was still uncivilized in its customs and in a savage state, and robbery was at that time still considered a most honorable occupation."

Chapter 4 – Roman Hispania

Caesar's Civil War

Prior to the time when Rome called itself an empire, Rome's government was known as the Roman Republic. The Romans had divided themselves into two political factions: the Optimates ("best ones") and the Populares ("favoring the people"). The Optimates were conservatives who basically favored the upper classes, as they believed they were the most qualified to run governmental affairs. The Populares were average citizens who felt that Rome and its colonies should be run by the people through its assemblies.

In 60 BCE, the First Triumvirate was established. This was an alliance between three notable politicians: Marcus Licinius Crassus, Gnaeus Pompeius Magnus (better known as Pompey), and Julius Caesar. After the death of Crassus in 53 BCE, the Triumvirate ended, as Caesar and Pompey were at odds with each other.

In 50 BCE, Caesar and Pompey warred with each other over control of Rome and its territories. Caesar was broadly supported by the Populares, while Pompey was supported by the Optimates.

The Crossing of the Rubicon

Rome had a law that governors and promagistrates had *imperium*, meaning "right to command," but only within the Roman provinces outside of Italy. There, they could march at the head of the army. *Imperium* was held by the elected magistrates and consuls of Italy alone. Governors and generals from other provinces could not march into Rome at the head of an army; their armies had to be disbanded beforehand. It was considered a capital offense not to do so.

The Rubicon River marked the northern border of Italy, and Caesar wanted to march his army into Rome in triumph. He was, after all, the governor of Cisalpine Gaul and had conquered the rest of Gaul in his earlier campaigns.

The ancient historian Suetonius indicated Caesar hesitated before boldly crossing the Rubicon, saying the immortal words, "The die has been cast." The date was January 10th, 49 BCE.

Pompey and his supporters fled Rome, including Titus Labienus, Caesar's former lieutenant. Labienus changed his allegiance to Pompey after Caesar crossed the Rubicon, as did Publius Attius Varus, who went back to his former post in Africa. Caesar, along with Mark Antony, pursued Pompey into Dyrrhachium across the Adriatic Sea and into Illyricum (today's Albania).

The Battle of Dyrrhachium

In July 48 BCE, Pompey's troops outnumbered those of Caesar. Pompey and his men managed to blockade Caesar, placing him in a terrible position. However, when his faithful friend, Mark Antony, counterattacked, it looked like Caesar was going to be successful. Due to Antony's skillful tactics, Pompey's forces became disorganized. Caesar had his right flank stand firm until it was clear they were horribly outnumbered and then ordered a retreat. Caesar lost between 1,000 to 4,000 men, and Pompey lost over 2,000.

The Battle of Pharsalus

In August 48 BCE, at Pharsalus in central Greece, Titus Labienus had his cavalry attack Caesar's cavalry at his left flank, pushing them back. However, Caesar had men hidden, and they suddenly raced forward. Pompey's cavalry panicked, and Caesar's men chased after them while they ran for the hills. The left wing of Pompey's forces remained, but they had no backup. So, Caesar's left wing swung around and went after them, and his third line of troops under Mark Antony assaulted the remainder of Pompey's men head-on. It was brutal, and all Pompey could do was retire from the battlefield and leave his troops in the center and the right to continue for as long as they could hold out.

Caesar had his men raid Pompey's camp. Pompey's auxiliaries in the camp defended it as best they could, but they couldn't last for long. Labienus fled to Corcyra, a Greek island. Pompey took his family, his gold, and cloak and went to Egypt.

Caesar left his legate, Quintus Cassius Longinus, in charge of Hispania and headed to other fronts that were more important in the context of the war, like Greece and Egypt. In September of 48 BCE, Pompey was assassinated in Egypt on Pharaoh Ptolemy XIII's orders. He thought it would gain Caesar's favor, but when Pompey's head was brought to Caesar, he was horrified. Some have wondered if he didn't manipulate the circumstances that led to Pompey's death, but most agree Caesar likely wouldn't have wanted Pompey to suffer such an inglorious insult by being beheaded.

During that time, Caesar increased the size of the Senate, so it could represent more people. He also regulated the distribution of grain, supported military veterans, reformed the tax codes, granted citizenship to people in Rome's many provinces, and even worked on creating the Julian calendar.

The Battle of Munda

In March 45 BCE, Caesar returned to Hispania and fought the Battle of Munda in southern Hispania Ulterior against Gnaeus Pompeius (also known as Pompey the Younger), the son of Pompey. Pompeius was joined by Titus Labienus and Publius Attius Varus.

The battlefield was on a slightly sloped hill. Caesar unsuccessfully tried to lure the Optimates down. Since that maneuver failed, he instead made a full-frontal assault. Caesar took command of his right wing and fought off the Pompeian right wing, weakening it. Pompeius had his generals dispatch some men from their left flank to strengthen his weak wing. That was a mistake, as Caesar then sent in his cavalry to attack the Pompeian rear. Labienus moved in some troops to intercept them, but the men in the center mistook that for a retreat. Labienus and Varus were both killed. The Pompeian forces broke up, and there was bedlam. Many fled to the city of Munda and were killed.

The Pompeian forces went on the run, pursued by Caesar and his men. Pompey's son was wounded and had to be carried on a litter near the lines of battle. He and his forces then took shelter near the town of Lauro.

The Battle of Lauro

At the Battle of Lauro, which was fought in early April of 45 BCE, some of the local people informed Caesar of the whereabouts of the Pompeian soldiers. Caesar's soldiers then surrounded them. The Pompeians were aided by uneven terrain, which allowed them to keep up their defensive attacks. The fighting was brutal, and the Pompeians incurred heavy casualties. Pompeius hid in a cave, but the locals informed Caesar of this, and they hunted him down. Caesar had him executed, and

Pompeius's head was severed from his body and displayed to the local people.

In 44 BCE, Julius Caesar was assassinated in Rome by his political rivals who feared his power. After all, he was declared dictator in perpetuity only a month before his death. He was succeeded by his adopted son, Octavian, who became the first emperor of Rome in 27 BCE.

The Cantabrian and Asturian Wars (29-19 BCE)

Throughout the early history of Hispania, there were troublesome tribes in the north. Among them were the Cantabrians and the Astures. Both of these tribes were from Celtic stock. They had spent the early times of Roman expansion in the Iberian Peninsula as mercenaries. During the Punic Wars, they fought on the side of the Carthaginians.

The ancient Roman historian Florus once wrote, "In the west almost all Spain had been subjugated except that part which adjoins the cliffs where the Pyrenees end and is washed by the nearer waters of the ocean." That was the land of the Cantabrian and Asturian tribes.

The Cantabrians and Astures were formidable enemies. When all was said and done, eight Roman legions had been sent to fight them, which numbered between 70,000 and 80,000 men.

In 29 BCE, the great Roman general Titus Statilius Taurus was sent to subdue those northern tribes. In 28 and 27 BCE, Sextus Appuleius II took over. When his term of duty was over, Appuleius returned to Rome and was celebrated in triumph.

In 27 BCE, Augustus made his debut as the commander of the ongoing war. Before going to Hispania, Augustus checked on the conditions in Gaul. He didn't reach Hispania until later in the year, reaching Tarraco (Tarragona) right before winter arrived. In 26 BCE, Augustus actually began to fight, setting up a three-pronged attack.

The first division attacked the Celtiberians at the city walls of Vellica, where they routed them. The enemy fled to Mount Vindius in the Cantabrian Mountains. Augustus's second division marched to Aracelium and wiped out the town. The third division went to Gallaecia in northwestern Hispania. The Cantabrians made their last stand at Mount Medullus. Augustus's soldiers dug a fifteen-mile ditch and put the area under siege. The Cantabrians knew that the Romans would either slaughter them or capture and sell them into slavery. They wanted to avoid that, preferring suicide to slavery. According to Florus, they vied with one another to hasten their deaths "in the midst of a banquet by fire and the sword and a poison which is there commonly extracted from the yew-tree." Many committed suicide rather than capitulate to the Romans. However, some preferred to live, and they surrendered to Augustus in person in 25 BCE.

The war was not over, though, for the Astures were not ready to capitulate. In 25 BCE, the Astures were encamped in the mountains, and they came down the slopes in droves. The Astures broke up their forces into three divisions to attack the Romans from their three encampments. The Astures' position and attack plans were betrayed by one of their subtribes, and Publius Carisius, who was in command of the Roman legions, was able to attack them by surprise.

Carisius attacked the Astures mercilessly. They resisted, but in the end, they were unable to repel the Romans. The Astures then fled to the fortified city of Lancia. Lancia permitted the Astures entry, but the Romans threatened to burn the city. The Asturian general begged mercy for his soldiers, indicating that Lancia would be a better monument to a Roman victory if left untouched. The Romans acceded and withdrew, knowing that they had won a psychological victory.

The war would continue on and off until 19 BCE, but the victory was already Augustus's by this point, and he annexed all of the Iberian Peninsula. Although minor rebellions would still occur, Augustus felt he had successfully pacified Hispania, and he made it his objective to introduce the region to the riches of Roman culture and society.

Pacification and Development

Even during the times when Rome suppressed the rebellions of the Hispanic tribes, its ultimate motivation was pacification and assimilation. Gradually, the Romans sent in their war veterans to work and populate the lands.

Miraculous Aqueduct at Augusta Emerita

I, Doalex, CC BY-SA 3.0 <http://creativecommons.org/licenses/by-sa/3.0/>, via Wikimedia Commons https://commons.wikimedia.org/wiki/File:El_acueducto_de_Los_Milagros.jpg

Augusta Emerita

The Romans established Augusta Emerita (today's Mérida, Spain) in central Hispania in 25 BCE. It was the capital of the province of Lusitania. Since they wanted to inculcate their settlers and the people of Hispania with Roman history, they built the Provincial Forum there in the 1st century CE. It had an adjoining temple to the goddess Diana. In addition, the Romans also erected a circus for chariot races. It could hold as many as 30,000 people.

Augusta Emerita was beautiful, but it was subject to droughts. Therefore, the Romans realized they had to build an aqueduct to supply the city and crops with water. This was called the *Acueducto de los Milagros* ("Miraculous Aqueduct"). It carried fresh water from the Proserpina Dam in Extremadura. Another dam, the Cornalvo Dam, was also constructed in Extremadura and is still being used today.

Asturica Augusta

In 14 BCE, the Romans established a city in the current province of León, in northwestern Hispania. Today, the city is called Astorga, and its name is derived from the Roman city, which they called Asturica, after the Astures, who lived there. During Roman times, the city provided an essential thoroughfare for the transport of copper from the mines of Rio Tinto in southwestern Hispania and silver from Emerita (Mérida).

Roman copper mine near the Rio Tinto River

Tarraco

Tarraco, modern-day Tarragona, was the oldest Roman town in the Iberian Peninsula, and it was the capital of Hispania Citerior in the 1st century BCE. The ancient writer Pomponius Mela described Tarraco as "the richest port on this coast." Located on the southeastern coast of Hispania on the Mediterranean Sea, Tarraco stands as a majestic memorial of the past.

The Arch of Berà in Tarragona (Tarraco)

Year of the dragon, CC BY-SA 3.0 <http://creativecommons.org/licenses/by-sa/3.0/>, via Wikimedia Commons https://commons.wikimedia.org/wiki/File:Spain.Catalonia.Roda.de.Bara.Arc.Bera.jpg

Under Caesar Augustus, the city flourished. He used Tarraco as a place to rest when in poor health. It was a bright sunny city, and when he was ill or during the winter months when he wasn't directing battles, he went there to rest.

Augustus rebuilt a road that had been originally put in by the Carthaginians and rerouted it to go from Narbo Martius (Narbonne) all the way to Gades (Cádiz) near the tip of southern Hispania. This was called the Via Augusta, and it was completed after Augustus's death in 14 CE.

During Augustus's reign, the city had an amphitheater and a provincial forum. Romans used slaves for gladiator combat in the amphitheaters. However, if soldiers lost battles, they were sometimes condemned to fight to the death in the arena. Romans could lose their status as free men for debt and petty crimes, and they, too, were forced into the arenas. Other gladiators volunteered for it, as gladiatorial combat could make a strong man very wealthy.

Today, Tarraco is one of the largest archaeological sites in Spain and is a World Heritage Site.

Baelo Claudia

Located just near the tip of Hispania and Gibraltar, this town was very wealthy, as it was able to benefit from the commerce on the Mediterranean Sea and the eastern Atlantic Ocean. The height of its importance was reached during the 2nd century CE, but it fell into disuse because of a number of earthquakes in the several centuries that followed.

The city was noted for its tuna fishing. In Baelo Claudia, "garum" was made. This was a fermented fish sauce with a savory taste. It was popular not only in Rome but also in the previous Hispanic colonies of the Phoenicians. It was manufactured in various grades, and the top residue, which was called *allec*, was spooned off and given to the poor to flavor their farina, which was a type of flour they used for their food.

Panorama of Baelo Claudia

Although it seems pedestrian, garum was a popular product and a major export. In time, it became a staple in Roman cuisine. Garum was also modified to make liquamen, which was also quite nutritious. The Romans used it to feed their soldiers. Since one of the ingredients was sea salt, it acted as an effective preservative for fish. Sometimes, it was used for medicinal purposes.

Roman Bridges

Many of the rivers in Hispania were wide, so the Romans built grand stone bridges over the major rivers. These bridges were attractive; many arches were used for support, and the pillars in the water at each end of the arches were heavily reinforced.

The ancient Romans used segmental arches in the construction of the supports for the bridges. The segmental arch was less than 180°. It added more height to the lower portion to compensate for flooding. Other bridges had larger arches, like the one pictured below. They were quite beautiful, and many still stand today as a testament to the architectural skills of the ancient Romans.

The Alcántara Bridge in Extremadura
Dantla at the German-language Wikipedia, GFDL <http://www.gnu.org/copyleft/fdl.html>, via Wikimedia Commons https://commons.wikimedia.org/wiki/File:Bridge_Alcantara.JPG

Caesaraugusta

Caesaraugusta, today known as Zaragoza, located in northeastern Hispania, had been populated by the Sedetani tribe. The Romans founded a city there for the war veterans from the Cantabrian Wars. It is not known when exactly it was founded, but it is believed to have been built between 25 and 11 BCE.

The Romans built a magnificent theater nearby. Greek and Roman plays were performed there, mostly tragedies and comedies. Roman comedies depended upon stock characters, one or more of whom would be the protagonist in the play:

the *adulescens* – a single man in his late teens

the *leno* – a character who was immoral

the *senex* – a parent concerned with his relationship with his son, who gets involved in poor or illicit relationships

the *parasitus* –a nuisance, as the term implies

the *miles gloriosus* – an arrogant character, a braggart

the *virgo* – an innocent young maiden

the *matrona* – the mother or wife who interferes with her children's lives

Amphitheater at Caesaraugusta
https://commons.wikimedia.org/wiki/File:Teatro_Romano_Cesaraugusta-vista_desde_arriba-3.jpg

The amphitheaters were also used for civic celebrations, which were intended to impress the Hispanic population with Roman sophistication and power. It was considered a sign of status if a town had its own amphitheater.

Romanization of Hispania

The architects of Hispania themselves started to design their own towns after the Roman style. They built public buildings and even bathhouses for their own people. After a community would do this, the Romans awarded the town with the status of *municipium*, which gave the people of the city the "Latin right," meaning they had extra privileges. Those practices accelerated under the reigns of Emperors Vespasian (69-79 CE), Titus (79- 81 CE), Domitian (81-96 CE), and Hadrian (117-138 CE).

Vespasian extended the privileges of the Latin right to all the communities of Hispania, although there were some who didn't conform, like a community near Seville, where archaeologists discovered bronze tablets with orders issued by Emperor Domitian for the people to conform to the Roman customs and laws.

Most of the privileges the native (Hispanic) communities received most likely only applied to the elites of the districts, as no mention was made of the lower classes.

When the uprisings later decreased, the number of Roman legions serving in Hispania was gradually reduced. By Vespasian's reign, there was only one Roman legion left, and it served in today's province of León.

Religion

The Roman deities started to be assimilated into the pagan belief system of the early Hispanics. In Gades (Cádiz), a blend of Hercules, the great Roman god, and Melqart, the Phoenician goddess of the sea, was manifested in a cult built up around the two.

In the 1ˢᵗ century, Christianity began taking root in Hispania. In 286 CE, Diocletian split the empire into two sectors: the Eastern Roman Empire and the Western Roman Empire. During the reigns of Diocletian and Maximian, as well as Galerius and Constantius Chlorus, who followed, edicts were passed that required Christians to obey traditional Roman statutes. Those laws stated that people were to return to the worship of the Roman gods.

Constantine I, also known as Constantine the Great, became the emperor in 306, and he would later go on to reunite the Roman Empire. In 313 CE, he legalized the Christian religion, and on his deathbed in 337, he became the first Roman emperor to convert to Christianity.

Chapter 5 – Enter the Germanic Tribes and the Muslims

During the early 5th century, the Visigoths, a Germanic tribe, migrated westward through Europe. When the Roman Empire was invaded by the Vandals, Alans, and Suebi, Rome asked King Wallia of the Visigoths for military assistance. The Visigoths were then made *foederati* of Rome, meaning that this assistance would result in benefits for the Visigoths.

The Fall of the Roman Empire

In 409 CE, the Vandals crossed the Pyrenees and started settling in Hispania. Two of their sub-tribes, the Hasdingi and Silingi, settled in Hispania after receiving land grants from Rome in exchange for their military assistance. At this point, Rome started losing control of Hispania.

The Suebi tribes under King Rechiarius invaded Hispania. By 432, the Suebi had ravaged Hispania and controlled most of the peninsula.

In 456, King Theodoric II of the Visigoths defeated Rechiarius near Astorga in northwestern Hispania. His troops then sacked several Suebi towns and massacred many people. After that, Theodoric took over Hispania Baetica in the southwest and part of Hispania Lusitania.

In 466, Euric rose to the Visigothic throne. He attempted to consolidate the Iberian Peninsula. He took the rest of Hispania Lusitania and captured Hispania Tarraconensis by 472.

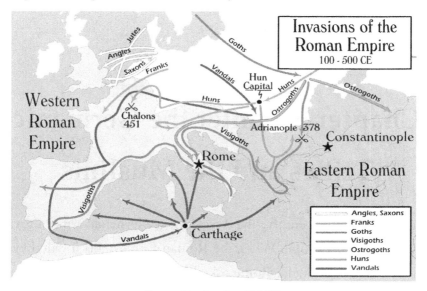

Roman Empire circa 500 CE

Two years later, Julius Nepos became the de facto Western Roman emperor. In 475, he was usurped by Orestes, the top military commander of the Roman forces. Orestes then crowned his sixteen-year-old son, Romulus Augustus, the next emperor of Rome. His *foederati* demanded they be given a third of the land in Italy. Orestes refused, and when they rose up against him, Orestes fled. The tribes had appointed an officer named Odoacer as their king, who chased down Orestes and killed him. The sixteen-year-old Romulus was dragged before Odoacer, where he surrendered his throne. Odoacer looked down upon the boy, and in a compassionate gesture, he allowed Romulus to settle in Campania in Italy. According to the legend, what became the great Roman Empire was founded by a boy named Romulus. In 476, it was ended by a boy named Romulus.

Romulus Augustulus surrendering to the Germanic chieftain Odoacer
https://commons.wikimedia.org/wiki/File:Young_Folks%27_History_of_Rome_illus420.png

Visigothic Rule

The Visigoths then controlled all of Iberia. In around 589, the Visigoths converted to Christianity. In 654, the Visigothic king, Recceswinth, published a law code named *Liber Iudiciorum*, also known as the Visigothic Code. Prior to this code, Iberia had different laws for Romans and Visigoths, but King Recceswinth eliminated these legal and social distinctions. *Liber Iudiciorum* united various aspects of the tribal codes, Catholic law, and Roman law.

The Visigoths placed their capital in the Kingdom of Toledo. In 574, the Visigothic king, Liuvigild, fought against the Cantabrians and established the Duchy of Cantabria. In 578, King Liuvigild built the city of Reccopolis in central Iberia, doing so in the Byzantine style of eastern Europe. It contained a grand palace, a mine, and a church.

Basilica and grounds at Reccopolis

Borjaanimal, CC BY-SA 3.0 ES <https://creativecommons.org/licenses/by-sa/3.0/es/deed.en>, via Wikimedia Commons https://commons.wikimedia.org/wiki/File:Recopolis_-_Basilica_(Exterior).jpg

One of the areas that were left unmolested by the Romans was the land of the Basques. They lived in the upper northeastern area of Iberia in the mountains of the Pyrenees. Up until then, the land of the Basques was used as a crossroads for Europe. The Visigoths, though, wanted to conquer and control them. For over two centuries, the Basques and the Visigoths fought battle after battle. Those attacks tended to make the Basques unite more closely, and they fought to preserve their language, *Euskara,* and their culture. In fact, the Basques even held on to their old nature religion for many years.

During this time, education spread throughout Iberia, led by scholars such as Bishop Isidore of Seville, an expert in etymology; Eugenius I of

Toledo, who was skilled in mathematics and astronomy; Theodulf of Orléans, a poet and theologian; and King Sisebut of the Visigoths, who was a poet.

Goldsmiths of the Visigothic Era

In times past, the term "Visigoths" was associated with barbarianism. However, the art and jewelry of the Visigoths show a great deal of artistry and professional skill. Two of the most prized pieces from that era are votive crowns. They are made of gold and interspersed with precious stones, such as sapphires and pearls, among others.

Eagle-shaped brooches called fibulae demonstrate the delicate work performed by master goldsmiths. These were found in necropolises belonging to noble families.

Symbols of military rank were visible in a soldier's belt buckle, and they were imitations of the Byzantine style. They were decorated with lapis lazuli, a semi-precious stone.

The Visigothic architecture in their churches followed the traditional cruciform pattern, and some churches were built upon the foundations of old Roman buildings, like the Church of Santa María de Melque, for example. Later on, the Knights Templar, one of the organizations that aided in the Crusades, cleverly converted the dome of the church into a turret for defensive purposes. Horseshoe-shaped arches were developed by Visigothic artisans, and they supported the vault under the overhead apse.

Religion

Contrary to popular opinion, the Visigoths were Christians. However, they followed Arianism, which promoted the doctrine that Jesus Christ is a distinct entity from God the Father and is subordinate to Him. This strand of Christianity was promoted by Arius, a presbyter in Alexandria. Catholicism rejected that belief as heresy. Many Visigoths later converted to Catholicism. There was some friction between the Visigoths and the Catholics in Iberia, but those conversions helped ease the tension between them.

Umayyad Conquest

The Muslim Umayyad Caliphate (661–750) engaged in conquests like the caliphates before it, incorporating North Africa, among other areas. In 710, Musa bin Nusayr, the ruler of Muslim North Africa, dispatched Tariq ibn Ziyad to raid Iberia. He took mostly Berbers along with him, although there were some Arab warriors as well.

The Berbers were from North Africa (namely Morocco, Tunisia, and Algeria), and they were Islamic converts. The non-Muslim community called them the "Moors," named after the country of Mauretania, in northwestern Africa, where they came from. In time, the Moors came to represent Muslim inhabitants in the Iberian Peninsula and elsewhere in Europe.

The Battle of Guadalete

Tariq sailed for Gibraltar and confronted the troops of King Roderick of the Visigoths, who was returning from an engagement with the Basques. The two armies met at Guadalete, which is thought to have been near Cádiz, on the western shore of Iberia. Although the numbers of warriors participating may not be accurate, primary sources state that Roderick had 100,000 warriors and Tariq had 187,000. The Visigoths engaged in a number of very violent hit-and-run raids, never attacking with full force. That gave the Muslims an opening, and King Roderick was slain early in the battle. It was a brutal, bloody battle. The Visigothic casualties were not recorded, while one chronicler estimates the Muslims suffered 3,000 dead. More contemporary historians indicate that treachery had caused Roderick to lose control. The defeat of the Visigothic army essentially left Iberia open for invasion.

After the rule of the Visigoths, the assimilation of the Visigoths and Hispano-Romans occurred at a fast pace. The nobility thought of themselves as the "Hispani" or the "gens Gothorum" and thought of themselves as one people. Some of them fled to Asturias or Septimania.

In the mountain areas of the Cantabrian and Pyrenees Mountains, the Cantabrians, Astures, Basques, and the people from western Galicia remained unassimilated. The territories around the Pyrenees, in particular, continued to resist assimilation into the cultures of their conquerors.

The Muslims generally left the non-Muslims alone to practice their own religion, but they did treat them as second-class citizens, insisting that they pay a special tax called the jizya.

In 713, Abd al-Aziz ibn Musa took control of the territory occupied by the Visigothic governor Theodemir, who was living in southeastern Iberia with his followers. The Muslims permitted him to establish an autonomous kingdom there, but it functioned as a client state, and they, too, paid the jizya.

In 714, the Muslim commander Musa Ibn Nusayr marched up the Ebro River to take on the western Basque territories and the tribes in the Cantabrian Mountains. It was reported he had little or no opposition in these regions. However, the far northern areas weren't their main focus, as the mountains were steep and inhospitable. The Muslims managed to reach the city of Pamplona in 714. The Basques in that city submitted after hammering out a compromise with the invaders.

Internal Conflicts between the Moors and Arab Factions

When Arab Muslims settled in parts of Iberia, there were ethnic tensions between them and the Moors from North Africa. The Arab Muslims attempted to place the jizya on them, and rebellions broke out, first in North Africa and then in Iberia. In 740, the inhabitants gave up their garrisons in León, Astorga, and other northwestern territories.

In 750, the Umayyad dynasty was overthrown by the Abbasids. However, the Umayyads would not sit still for too long. In 756, Abd al-Rahman I, a prince from the deposed Umayyad dynasty, seized power in Córdoba, establishing the Emirate of Córdoba. This allowed Muslim power in al-Andalus to stabilize. In 778, he campaigned in Zaragoza in northeastern Iberia and gained a measure of control there. He also gained control of Pamplona and the Basque lands in 781.

The aristocrats of al-Andalus embraced Islam in order to maintain power, but the majority of the population were Christians.

In the 10th century, al-Rahman's descendant, Abd al-Rahman III, declared that he alone was the caliph of Córdoba and severed all loyalties to the Syrian and Egyptian caliphates. He was more interested in maintaining his power base in North Africa, but he was unable to do so and remained isolated from the Muslim world.

Death in the Name of Religion

Abu Amir Muhammad ibn Abdullah ibn Abi Amir al-Ma'afiri, better known as Almanzor, became the chancellor of the Caliphate of Córdoba in the 10th century. He was essentially the ruler of Iberia, as the caliph was young, inexperienced, and weak, but Almanzor never ruled in name. Almanzor made it his objective to see that all of Iberia recognize his sovereignty. In 977, he started conducting military campaigns, which became more frequent and violent as he gained more power. Although they disagree as to the details, historians estimate that he conducted assaults on Christian areas in Iberia about fifty-six times, killing and slashing Christians as he raged through the country. That generated a state of insecurity, and Christians took refuge in fortified towns and castles. Almanzor mercilessly plundered the Christian areas, but he didn't occupy the areas he assaulted. Thus, most people returned when he left, which prevented long-term ruin.

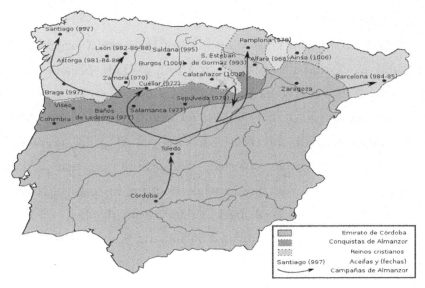

Major campaigns of Almanzor

Redtony, CC BY-SA 3.0 <https://creativecommons.org/licenses/by-sa/3.0>, via Wikimedia Commons https://commons.wikimedia.org/wiki/File:Map_Almanzor_campaigns-es.svg

In 985, Almanzor sacked the city of Barcelona. In 988 and 989, he and his troops assaulted Zamora, Toro, Astorga, and León in northwestern Iberia.

Military campaigns of Almanzor

https://en.wikipedia.org/wiki/Almanzor#/media/File:Map_Almanzor_campaigns-es.svg

As noted in the map, the Muslims essentially had control of nearly all of Hispania, with the exception of the northern areas. Those continued to be controlled by the Christians.

Battle of Religions

In 929, the Caliphate of Córdoba fell apart. The former caliphate was broken up into taifas, which were independent entities in the Iberian Peninsula. The leaders of these principalities often raided Christian lands and carried Christians away to serve as slaves. The taifas then started fighting with each other, becoming weaker as a result.

The Siege of Toledo

In 1085, the Christian king Alfonso VI of León and Castile found an opportunity to expand his lands when Yahya al-Qadir became the new leader of the Taifa of Toledo. He wanted Alfonso's help in putting down an uprising, but instead of that, Alfonso took Toledo for himself. Alfonso agreed to award al-Qadir the control of Valencia. Al-Qadir accepted, but some of the local people objected. Throughout the years, Alfonso continued to expand his territories while ensuring his control remained strong. In 1099, Alfonso took back Valencia with the help of El Cid. During this time, Alfonso repopulated Salamanca, Segovia, and Ávila with Christians.

The taifas grew concerned when the Christians started gaining territory in Hispania. They called upon the Almohad Caliphate, a Berber Muslim empire in North Africa, to help. The founder of the Almohads, Ibn Tumart, was a Muslim scholar. His was a school of Islam that adopted what was called the "Ash'ari" school. It ascribes to Sunni Islam, but it contains a mixture of other beliefs as well. The Ash'ari school maintains a very orthodox approach to Islam and still exists today.

Battle of Alarcos

The Almohads, under Abu Yusuf Ya'qub al-Mansur, fought for control of the province of Castile in 1195 against King Alfonso VIII of Castile. Alfonso underestimated the strength of the Muslim forces. During the battle, Alfonso's cavalry became disordered, and they were almost completely surrounded and were virtually destroyed as a result. Castile then lost control of the area, and nearby castles were surrendered or abandoned.

The battle against the Muslims in Iberia took on a religious significance. The papacy justified war against the Muslim invaders, saying it was in defense of Christianity, as they considered the Muslims to be "infidels." Christian groups called "orders" were founded to combat this threat, such as the Order of Santiago, the Order of Calatrava, the Order of Montesa, the Order of Alcántara, and the Knights Templar.

The Battle of Las Navas de Tolosa

This battle took place in July 1212 in southern Iberia. Alfonso VIII of Castile was aided by soldiers from the Christian Kingdom of Navarre, which was led by Sancho VII, and King Peter II of Aragon. They surprised the Almohads at their camp and raided it. According to legend, during the attack, they came upon the tent of the caliph himself, Muhammad al-Nasir. The caliph escaped, but many Muslims were slain. Christian domination was secured after this battle.

Repossession of Spain

While the Muslims were trying to hold on to the southern areas of Spain, the Spanish provinces in the north were being integrated into Christian territories. They then started using the word "Spain," taken from the Castilian word *España*, to refer to themselves and again reestablished their provincial borders.

The Kingdom of Asturias was willed to Fruela II in 910 after the death of his father, Alfonso III. The Kingdom of Asturias transitioned into the Kingdom of León in 924 when Fruela II became the king of León.

Around 1230, the Kingdom of León and the Kingdom of Castile were merged when Ferdinand III of Castile was bequeathed the Kingdom of León. This laid the foundation for the Crown of Castile, which was a polity that combined the two powerful territories.

The Kingdom of Navarre had been stabilized and was ruled by Sancho VII in the early 13th century.

The Kingdom of Aragon was led by King James I in the early 13th century. Remnants of the Almohad warriors from the campaigns of

Almanzor occupied the Balearic Islands, off the coast of Spain. James and Spanish allies from Catalonia took troops to the island of Majorca to expel the Muslims. In 1229, they tried to reconquer Majorca but didn't succeed until 1231.

By 1250, the taifas were in decline, and the repopulation of the Christians started in the northern Douro River Valley in central Spain, part of the Ebro River Valley running from northeastern Spain diagonally into the Mediterranean, and the central segment of Catalonia in the eastern area. The southern area below the Douro River was resettled by Christians during the following two centuries.

The *Fueros*

A *fuero*, or "charter," was a set of laws and privileges that was usually regionally based and was intended for a certain group of people. For some regions, it had the weight of a constitution. The term was first used during the Middle Ages and referred to the body of regulations and rewards or easements granted by a monarch. In exchange, the peasants agreed to defend the land for the monarch or church official in the case of church property.

As peasants returned to the land, they claimed areas that were suitable for farming. Once that occurred, the population of the provinces grew, and commerce abounded.

The establishment of the *fueros* laid the foundation for modern Spain's autonomous communities.

The Last Muslim Holdout

The final holdout for Muslim power in Spain was the Emirate of Granada in the far south. It lasted well into the 15th century, dissolving in 1492. By then, the dawn of Habsburg Spain was just on the horizon.

Chapter 6 –The Transformation of Spain

The 14th and 15th centuries proved to be a pivotal period in Spain. It marked the critical difference between what was and what was to come.

The Battle of Vega de Pagana

The Battle of Vega de Pagana was fought in 1339. It was the battle for the conquest of Granada, the last Muslim stronghold in Spain. It pitted King Alfonso XI of Castile with his Order of Alcantara against Abu Malik, the son of the sultan of Morocco, Abu al-Hasan Ali, and his troops. Abu Malik's father had kept the peace signed in 1334, but he wanted to expand.

Historians have little details as to the logistics of the battle, but Abu Malik was killed.

Battle of Río Salado and the Spanish/Muslim Campaign at Gibraltar

In late 1340, Abu al-Hasan, the sultan of Morocco, receive an appeal from Sultan Yusuf I of Granada to help drive out the Castilians. The Muslims assembled their fleet under the command of Muhammad ibn Ali al-Azafi.

The Castilian fleet met the Muslims at the Castilian outpost of Gibraltar, where they were met by forty-four galleys under the command of Admiral Alfonso Jofre de Tenorio. Al-Azafi surrounded them, and Tenorio was killed.

Thinking that it would take the Castilians a long time to rebuild their fleet, Abu Hasan placed a siege on Tarifa near Cádiz. Believing he had time, Abu Hasan sent some of al-Azafi's galleys back, leaving only twelve for himself.

Alfonso XI sought the aid of the king of Aragon and King Afonso IV of Portugal. In addition, they swiftly constructed extra ships at Seville and moved them in place to block any supply lines to the Muslims. With 20,000 Castilian, Aragonese, and Portuguese on their way, Abu Hasan lifted the siege and moved up on a hill between Tarifa and the sea. Yusuf I, Sultan of Granada, placed his forces on a hill nearby. During the night, Alfonso XI reinforced his garrison at Tarifa, meeting only slight resistance from a light Muslim cavalry. Abu Hasan's Muslim scouts either failed to see that the city was being reinforced or were afraid of admitting it. This would be a serious mistake.

King Alfonso XI, who led the main force of Castilian fighters, decided he would attack Abu Hasan's main troops, while Afonso IV of Portugal would take on Yusuf's Granada forces. The Orders of Alcántara and Calatrava bolstered up the Portuguese. After much effort, the Spanish forces aided the vanguard troops in crossing the Salado River.

Afonso ordered a full-scale attack with just himself and his troops. However, the rearguard arrived on the scene just in time to help, attacking the Muslim forces from the rear. The Muslims broke rank and fled toward the city of Algeciras. The entire battle took just three hours.

The Muslims ran to the Guadamecí River, and the Spanish pursued them. There, the Spanish raided their camp, even taking hostages and prisoners, included females. Some of the sultan's wives were even killed.

Siege of Algeciras

Algeciras was just a short bay away from the tip of Gibraltar. The Muslims had been routed from their strongholds north of there during the Battles of Vega de Pagano and Río Salado. The survivors had retreated to the fortifications at Algeciras.

Alfonso XI placed a siege upon the Algeciras Muslim stronghold in 1342, and he received side from Juan Núñez III de Lara and a number of other Spanish fighters. Alfonso divided their forces between three men: Don Juan Manuel, Pedro Fernández de Castro, and Juan Núñez himself. After nearly two years, the Muslims finally surrendered.

The Fifth Siege of Gibraltar

As one might expect by the name, this was the fifth time the Spanish and the Muslims fought over Gibraltar in a span of forty years. They staged a long siege and dug defensive ditches all around it, as well as across the isthmus to blockade the Muslims from accessing supplies and reinforcements.

The siege continued on during the fall and winter, but there was still no indication that the garrison would surrender. Suddenly, the Black Death hit. It infiltrated the Castilian camp, and many died. However, Alfonso was determined and hung on. Then King Alfonso himself was struck with the plague. He died on Good Friday, March 26th, 1350. His forces notified Yusuf I, the sultan of Granada, who was commanding the Muslim forces there. He courteously permitted the Spanish soldiers to leave as they carried the body of their deceased king.

Peter of Castile

In 1350, Alfonso XI was succeeded by his son, Peter. Peter was then declared Peter I, King of Castile and León. Peter's mother was Maria of Portugal. He was under the firm hand of his mother until he was encouraged to free himself from her influence by the powerful noble Juan Alfonso de Albuquerque.

Peter was a good-looking young man, and it is said that he secretly married lovely María de Padilla, who was being raised in Albuquerque's household. She convinced Peter to rid himself of Albuquerque's influence, placing him back under the influence of his mother and the other nobles. Not knowing of his marriage to María, Peter's mother and the court nobles convinced Peter to marry Blanche of Bourbon in 1353.

Peter deserted Blanche but pursued his relationship with María, with whom he had had four children.

The War of the Two Peters and the Castilian Civil War

This war, as one might have guessed, involved two Peters: Peter I, King of Castile, and Peter IV, King of Aragon. Peter of Aragon supported the accession of Henry of Trastámara, who was the illegitimate son of Alfonso XI and his mistress, Eleanor de Guzmán. Peter of Castile, on the other hand, was the legitimate son of Alfonso XI.

In 1357, the Castilians conquered Tarazona in Aragon, which was followed by a temporary truce. In 1361, the war broke out again. Queen Blanche had been imprisoned so she could be out of the way for Peter to enjoy his other dalliances, but Peter still seemed to see her as a threat. Although it is not known for certain, some believe Peter had her executed. This is just one of the reasons why Peter was called "Peter the Cruel" by his contemporaries.

The fighting between the two Peters resumed. The Castilians captured the fortresses at Verdejo, Alhama, and Torrijos, among other places. However, a new peace was soon arranged, and all those conquered forts were returned to their owners.

In the following year, Peter of Castile called upon Charles II of Navarre, Edward III of England, and Edward's son, who was known as Edward the Black Prince. Peter of Castile then caught Peter of Aragon off guard and conquered Arize, Atece, Terrer, Moros, Cetina, and Alhama. After this, Peter of Castile went back to Seville.

The hostilities continued, and in 1366, Henry Trastámara, who was in France, gathered a large army of Aragonese nobles and English mercenaries. He had the support of the kings of both Aragon and France, Peter IV and Charles V, respectively. With this alliance, Henry invaded Castile, causing Peter to flee.

Peter of Castile did not want to go out without a fight, and he called upon his supporter, the Black Prince, for aid, promising the prince some lands in Castile. The Black Prince was pleased with this arrangement and brought along some English mercenaries with him.

At the Battle of Nájera in 1367, Edward the Black Prince restored Peter to the throne. However, Peter didn't keep his promise and never paid Edward for his service. Edward's health was poor, and he soon left the Iberian Peninsula.

That was the signal for Henry Trastámara to return. In 1368, he did so, and the Cortes of Burgos recognized him as the king of Castile. Peter, though, did have some supporters, and eventually, there was nothing left to do but decide who the ruler would be on the battlefield. In 1369, the Battle of Montiel was waged. Their forces confronted each other, and Peter was ultimately slain.

Death of "Peter the Cruel"
https://commons.wikimedia.org/wiki/File:Pierre_leCruel.jpg

Henry Trastámara then became Henry II, King of Castile in 1369.

The Fernandine Wars and Treaty of Salvaterra

After the death of Peter of Castile and the accession of Henry Trastámara to the Castilian throne, Portugal and the Kingdom of Castile fought, as the Portuguese believed Ferdinand had the right to the throne. The two nations had three conflicts over this: one from 1369 to 1370, the second from 1372 to 1373, and the last from 1381 to 1382. In 1383, King Ferdinand I of Portugal and Henry II of Castile signed the Treaty of Salvaterra de Magos, which delineated the following principles:

The separation of the Kingdom of Portugal from the Kingdom of Castile unless otherwise stipulated by the Cortes of Spain.

Beatrice, Ferdinand's daughter, was recognized as the "king" of Portugal, and Ferdinand was the "king consort" unless Ferdinand had male heirs.

The throne of Portugal would be bequeathed to the offspring of Beatrice and her husband.

The throne would go to John of Castile, son of Henry Trastámara and his offspring if Beatrice had no children.

Queen Leonor Telles de Menezes would remain regent of the kingdom if Ferdinand had no heirs and if Beatrice didn't have a male child who reached fourteen years of age.

John II of Castile

John was the son of King Henry III of Castile. His mother was the granddaughter of the infamous King Peter "the Cruel." John's reign started in 1406, but he was underage, so his regents ran the kingdom. While they were in charge, they passed the Valladolid laws in 1411, which stipulated that Jews had to wear certain clothing and couldn't hold public office. When he came of age in 1418, John married Maria of Aragon. Of his first four children, only one survived infancy, Henry IV, who succeeded him.

The First Battle of Olmedo

Maria of Aragon died in 1445. During that year, the Battle of Olmedo was fought over the levying of rents from Medina del Campo. These had to be paid directly to John II of Castile instead of John II of Aragon, whom the people felt had the right to them. John II of Castile prevailed in that battle.

John II remarried in 1451, this time to Queen Isabella of Portugal. They had two children, Isabella and Alfonso. John would die in 1454, a year after Alfonso was born.

Young Isabella's half-brother, Henry IV of Castile, was in charge of her when he took the throne, but he didn't take care of her or her brother, Alfonso, very well, despite the fact that her father had arranged this for them. The conditions in their castle at Arévalo were poor.

In 1462, Isabella and Alfonso were taken into the household of King Henry's wife, Joan of Portugal, and Alfonso was given a tutor. Isabella's living conditions were much improved. She was dressed well and had a full education.

In 1467, the nobles in the kingdom insisted that Henry's younger half-brother, Alfonso, be named as his successor if he married Joanna la Beltraneja, whose paternity they questioned. It was believed that Henry was impotent and that Joanna was the daughter of the powerful noble, Beltrán de la Cueva.

The Second Battle of Olmedo

Henry tried to support his daughter's claim. The supporters of Alfonso and Henry's forces clashed at the Second Battle of Olmedo in 1467. Even though Henry's troops were superior in strength, the outcome was undecided. However, Henry agreed to the legitimacy of Alfonso if he married Joanna, but the whole issue became moot when Alfonso died in 1468. Some say it was by poisoning, but it was more likely from the plague or consumption (tuberculosis), which was a very common disease during the Middle Ages.

Ferdinand II and Isabella

Isabella, who had been sitting on the sidelines at this point, came into play. Since she was the half-sister of Henry IV, the Spanish legislative committee, the Cortes, decided that Isabella would inherit the throne after his death. In 1469, she married Ferdinand II, the son of John II of Aragon, which means the two were second cousins. They would become known as the Catholic Monarchs.

War of Castilian Succession

Henry IV died in December of 1474. Joanna la Beltraneja claimed she was entitled to the throne of Castile because she was the reputed daughter of Henry IV. She married King Afonso V of Portugal, who was her uncle, in 1475.

The Siege of Burgos

This siege took place between 1475 and early 1476. Afonso V had his troops entrench themselves at the old castle in the city of Burgos, as it wasn't currently used by the Castilian monarchs. However, King Afonso had priorities in Zamora, so he left Burgos behind in early December. During the course of the siege, Ferdinand II had his troops cut the supply lines and sever the water tunnels. Despite their difficulties, the troops sequestered there held out for nine months, but they eventually surrendered.

The Battle of Toro

At the Battle of Toro in March of 1476, Prince John, the son of Afonso V, practically annihilated the right wing of the Castilian troops. However, the Castilian commanders, the duke of Alba and Cardinal Mendoza, beat the left-center of Afonso's army. Mendoza was strictly a military man; he was just a prelate in name only.

Each side defeated half of the troops of their opposition. Both sides claimed victory, but military analysts indicated the outcome in this battle was undecided. Politically, though, it was a win for Isabella, as the vast majority of Portuguese troops returned home.

Naval Battles

The Portuguese were considered experts in sailing the Mediterranean, as well as around the northern and western coasts of Africa. In May of 1476, the Catholic Monarchs found out that the Portuguese had richly laden cargo ships on their way to Portugal. The Castilians then dispatched five caravels and five galleys to confront them. The Castilians attacked the Portuguese ships near Cádiz, on the southwestern coast of Spain, and damaged their fleet.

The Castilians, under Carlos de Valera, sailed to the Cape Verde islands off the west coast of Africa, where they captured the notorious governor, António Noli, who was in the employ of Portugal.

France's Entry into the War

Once France heard of the succession dispute, it became interested in involving itself in the war and allied with Portugal. In 1476, the French attempted to enter Fuenterrabía (today's Hondarribia) in the Kingdom of Navarre in northern Spain. The Basque people lived there. They stood firmly on the side of Isabella and repelled the French. King Ferdinand was grateful and made arrangements to station his garrison at Pamplona, a major city in the Kingdom of Navarre.

In August of 1476, France sent a fleet under the privateer Guillaume Coulon, and Afonso V also sent two Portuguese galleys loaded with soldiers. Out at sea, the French managed to overcome the Spanish merchant ships from Cádiz. However, the French used incendiary weapons, which got out of control. As a result, the Portuguese galleys, as well as two of Coulon's ships, were destroyed in the conflagration.

Following that disaster, France withdrew any significant aid to Portugal, as their king, Louis XI, turned his attention to his struggles with the duke of Burgundy in France. Portugal and Castile, however, continued to fight.

The Treaty of Alcáçovas

In 1479, King Ferdinand and Queen Isabella signed a treaty with Afonso V and Prince John of Portugal. In it, the two nations agreed to respect each other's borders, and Afonso renounced any claim on the Crown of Castile. Joanna la Beltraneja was given two choices: 1) marry Isabella's one-year-old son, John, when he came of age if he consented to it, or 2) enter the convent. She chose the latter.

Another unresolved issue that was brought up had to do with the competition of Portugal and Spain over control of the eastern Atlantic.

The two countries discussed the status of the islands off the western coast of Africa. As a result of this treaty, it was agreed that Portugal would control Cape Verde, the Azores, and Madeira—islands that the Portuguese had historically inhabited. Portugal then agreed that Castile could have possession of the Canary Islands, whose ownership had been in dispute until then.

Toward the Homogeneity of Spain

Ferdinand's and Isabella's accession to the throne marked a time when Spain was attempting to unite the country. There were two issues that prevented this from happening: the Jewish and Muslim populations. Catholicism was one element common to both Aragon and Castile. In fact, all of Spain was predominately Catholic. This was one area that the nobles didn't disagree with the monarchs.

The Muslim Situation

The Muslim taifas, save for the province of Granada in southern Spain, had already disintegrated by this point. The Nasrid dynasty controlled the Muslim population in Granada from 1230 to 1492. Twenty-three emirs ruled it, and for ten years, the Christians and Muslims raided each other, especially on the borders. Battles usually broke out in the spring and let up in the winter. In 1478, a truce was signed by both parties.

The Granada War

In 1481, the Muslims staged a surprise attack on Zahara after the Christians raided their territories. The Muslims captured the town and marched the inhabitants into slavery. The Castilians then sent in a force and retook Zahara, as well as Alhama, which were both fortress towns. The sultan, Abu'l Hasan, attempted to retake Alhama but failed.

The Castilian forces next attempted to seize the town of Loja, but they weren't successful. Following that, Abu'l Hasan's son, Abu Abdallah, also known as Boabdil, styled himself as the new sultan in 1482, calling himself

Muhammad XII. At Lucena, the Christians captured Boabdil. In 1483, they designed a plot to rid Granada of the Muslims entirely. The monarchs released Boabdil, who was now their ally, to go to war against his father.

In 1485, Boabdil was expelled from his home base at Albayzín by his uncle, al-Zagal. Al- Zagal dethroned his elderly brother and took over Granada. His brother, Abu'l Hasan, died shortly afterward. Once al-Zagal was in total control, Boabdil then rushed to Ferdinand and Isabella for protection.

In the meantime, the marquis of Cádiz captured the town of Ronda in the western area of Granada. Boabdil was released from Ferdinand and Isabella's protection so he could continue his conquest of Granada. He promised limited independence to the Christians there and got the monarchs to make him a duke of any town he might capture.

The Siege of Málaga

In 1487, the Castilians placed the town of Vélez-Málaga under siege. Al-Zagal tried to respond, but he was slow to do so because of the internal civil war that raged between the Muslim factions. Ferdinand captured the town and discovered that it housed some Christian converts to Islam. This infuriated him, and he burned them alive. The rest of the inhabitants were enslaved. The Jews weren't harmed, as the Jewish populace from another region ransomed those who had been enslaved.

Boabdil took over Granada, Vélez-Rubio, Vélez-Blanco, and Vera in 1487. The Christians took some of Boabdil's land, but he didn't retaliate, as he assumed it would be returned to him later.

The Siege of Baza

Al-Zagal was still in control of the important stronghold of Baza. Although it was costly in terms of resources, in 1489, the Christians besieged Baza for six months. In 1490, Spain succeeded and captured al-

Zagal.

Boabdil was allowed to keep the city of Granada and was given land in the Alpujarra Mountains. He was unhappy with that, as the lands were administered by the Catholic Monarchs. In addition, Boabdil was heavily criticized by the Muslims in North Africa.

This land gave Boabdil no access to the sea, and therefore, he had no way to receive aid from the Muslim world. He was disgruntled with the arrangements and rebelled.

The Battle of Granada

In April 1491, the Catholic Monarchs sent their troops to Granada and placed the city under siege. The Muslim fighters argued with one another about what tactics to use, and many Muslims bribed the Castilians for relief. The Muslims attempted to surrender, but infighting occurred because of internal hostilities, causing delays. Finally, at the beginning of 1492, the city capitulated. Boabdil couldn't tolerate living in the mountains, and since he couldn't capture any more territory, he returned to Morocco.

The Jewish Situation

Jews had as much freedom to practice their religion as Christians in both Castile and Aragon. The situation wasn't the same across all of Spain, however. Prior to Ferdinand and Isabella's reign, there were many prejudicial practices in Spain, including persecution.

Ferdinand and Isabella were tolerant of the Jews, unlike many of the other European monarchs. Isabella, in particular, was protective of them. However, with the spread of Christianity, Catholicism, in particular, the monarchs planned on passing a decree that Spanish Jews must convert to Christianity. The Jewish converts were called *conversos,* and about 80,000 Jews converted during that time. Many people, though, felt that these conversions were insincere, so the prejudice against the Jews persisted.

Two prelates, Pedro González de Mendoza, Archbishop of Seville, and the Dominican Tomás de Torquemada, spoke to the monarchs about the severity of the matter and how it was leading to disunity. In response, Ferdinand and Isabella spoke to the pope.

The Alhambra Decree

After the Muslim threat had been overcome, the Spanish monarchs drew their attention to the Jewish population. Up until that time, Queen Isabella's confessor (a cleric who heard her confessions), Hernando de Talavera, suggested that she practice toleration. However, when a less tolerant confessor, Francisco Jiménez de Cisneros, took over, he advised her against that. She and Ferdinand then required that all Jews convert to Christianity and passed the Alhambra Decree to that effect in 1492. Unconverted Jews were permitted to take their belongings with them and were given a four-month window in which to do so. If they missed the deadline, they would be executed. Because of the rush to leave, they were forced to take only what they could carry. Many sold their more precious items to obtain more gold or silver. There was, therefore, an excess of goods on the market.

The Jews who emigrated were called "Sephardic Jews," and many moved to North Africa, where they were preyed upon by slave traders. North Africa was also undergoing a famine at the time, and some Jews returned to Spain and converted. Others settled in Portugal, Turkey, and the Balkans. Between 40,000 to 100,000 were expelled.

The Spanish Inquisition

During the Middle Ages, it was believed monarchs were given the power to rule by God. In order to increase their strength in Spain, King Ferdinand and Queen Isabella looked upon religion as the single immutable factor around which to create a unified country. The Spanish Inquisition, which was created in 1478, was used as a tool to create this unity. However, it often created disunity. The inquisitors targeted heretics, those who converted from Judaism or Islam to Christianity but didn't hold sincere beliefs. Neighbor would turn against neighbor, whether out of spite or greed, and many were accused of breaking the law.

Auto-da-fé, Death by Burning
See page for author, CC BY 4.0 <https://creativecommons.org/licenses/by/4.0>, via Wikimedia Commons https://commons.wikimedia.org/wiki/File:An_auto-da-f%C3%A9_of_the_Spanish_Inquisition_and_the_execution_o_Wellcome_V0041892.jpg

In 1490, two Jews and six *conversos* were picked up on charges of heresy and brought to the inquisitors. They had allegedly killed a Christian boy from the town of La Guardia. One of the accused, Yucef Franco, indicated that the *conversos* took a Christian boy to a cave and crucified him. Then he reported that they removed the boy's heart and drained it of blood. When all the prisoners were questioned, their stories didn't match. Investigators also indicated that there were no children missing from La Guardia. When they were informed of the supposed location of the body, none was found.

Rather than proclaim them innocent, the inquisitors assumed they were all lying and had them burned at the stake. Currently, some people still honor the boy who was supposedly killed in La Guardia. He is called the "Holy Child of La Guardia."

Motives Projected by Historians

There is no consensus among historians as to the motives of the Inquisition on the part of Ferdinand and Isabella. However, a cursory look at history appears to reveal some:

Create an atmosphere of unity through religion.

Weaken opposition to the Catholic Monarchs by strengthening their political authority.

Eliminate the *converso* minority and decrease the power of their influence.

Economic support. When one was imprisoned or sentenced for an offense, their property was confiscated by the state.

Chapter 7 – The Struggling Spanish Empire

Europe benefited from goods that were brought in from the "Indies," the term applied to Southeast Asia. During the 15th century, the caravans that traversed the old Silk Road declined with the rise of the Ottoman Empire in the East.

Spain had always competed with Portugal for domination of the maritime sea trade.

Bartholomew Diaz of Portugal discovered another way to the Indies, so Ferdinand and Isabella didn't want to fall behind. An explorer named Christopher Columbus approached the sovereigns for funding to make a voyage across the Atlantic Ocean to the Indies. Christopher and his brother, Bartholomew, had been turned down by other countries, including Portugal. Columbus, who was an excellent navigator and an even better marketer, approached Queen Isabella. He presented her his astronomical and cartography reports. Some scientists felt that Columbus had grossly underestimated the distance across the ocean. However, Isabella's clerk, Luis de Santángel, told the queen that another country might get there before Spain. This led Isabella and Ferdinand to agree to fund the voyage.

In 1492, Columbus and his crew set sail. After nearly two months on the Atlantic, Columbus landed on San Salvador. Columbus had landed on an island in the Bahamas, although he thought it was the Indies. The first people he encountered were the Taíno, Lucayan, and Arawak peoples. They were mostly naked, which made Columbus believe they were very poor. Columbus reported that they "ought to make good and skilled servants because they repeat very quickly whatever we say to them." He noted that the Arawak people had gold earrings and took them as prisoners until they could point out a source of the gold. He never found much of it, nor any of the precious stones he had hoped for. Columbus made three more voyages over the next decade, ending his travels in 1504.

The Niña, Pinta, and Santa María
https://commons.wikimedia.org/wiki/File:Gustav_Adolf_Closs_-_Die_Schiffe_des_Columbus_-_1892.jpg

When Europeans realized they had discovered a whole new land, the race was on. In 1498, Vasco da Gama reached India, although he went in the opposite direction as Columbus. It was Portugal, yet again, who succeeded in reaping the treasures from the great beyond.

In the meantime, Spain sent out its boldest explorers ever: the conquistadors. They discovered the gold that Spain had long searched for. The Spanish chronicler of these explorers, Bernal Díaz del Castillo, said, "When we saw so many cities and villages built in the water and other great towns on dry land we were amazed and said that it was like the enchantments...Some of our soldiers even asked whether the things we saw were but a dream."

The wonders of the Maya, Inca, and Aztec Empires opened up a treasure beyond what anyone had anticipated. The silver mines in the New World, particularly Mexico, spewed out wealth and overhauled the economy of Spain.

The New World and Its Exports

By the 16th century, Spain had settled colonies in the Netherlands, Belgium, and Luxembourg. In Mexico, Spain owned nearly one-half of the western portion of the New World and the western territories in South America. Spain was the largest empire in the world. In the New World, the Spanish created what it called New Spain, which was governmentally divided into captaincies. Mining efforts continued, which led to large Spanish settlements in Mexico. Cuba had been an important captaincy since the time of Columbus, as was Mexico, Peru, Chile, New Granada (current-day Columbia, Ecuador, and Venezuela), Rió de la Plata (Argentina and Uruguay), and Paraguay.

The two greatest exports from the Americas were silver and sugar. Those were labor-intensive endeavors, so the Spanish sent African slaves to do the heavy labor. They were taken from West Africa by slave traders, who shipped them over the Atlantic under deplorable conditions. The slaves that did survive were sold in slave markets in Brazil and the Spanish coastal colonies. Sugar had to be processed quickly, so plantations had their processing facilities on the same property.

The settlers created businesses to support the cities and towns. The indigenous farmers were given land to farm, and they paid tribute in the form of goods or labor for the Spanish populations. Very few rivers in New Spain were navigable, so early transport was done via mules or mule trains. One of the more exotic goods that were sold included cochineal, a red dye made from the bodies of certain insects that are found on nopal cactuses in Mexico and Central America. Vanilla beans were also grown, and it was quite popular in Europe, along with cacao. The cacao bean was harvested in Mexico, and contrary to what some might think, cacao is not naturally sweet. It has to be sweetened to be used as chocolate. The Catholic Church benefited from cacao production, as it was the most valuable contributor to the tithe, the tax that was charged on certain goods. The most popular alcoholic beverages were rum, which is made from molasses derived from the sugar-making process; chicha, a corn beer; and pulque, which is made from the agave plant in South America.

There was little that Spanish America could offer in terms of textiles, so they made most of their own clothing out of local wool. That, of course, couldn't be used for the export market.

The Habsburg Dynasty

Isabella and Ferdinand heralded from the House of Trastámara. They realized they could secure the Spanish succession by associating Spain with the power of the great families of Europe. The Habsburgs were one of the most distinguished royal houses, having been in existence since the 11th century. In 1496, their daughter, Joanna, was married to Philip the Fair, a member of the Habsburg dynasty. Isabella and Ferdinand's son John married Margaret of Austria in order to reinforce the royal line with the Habsburg lineage. Maria, Isabella and Ferdinand's fourth child, married Manual I of Portugal to further strengthen their alliance with mighty Portugal; before this, Manuel had been married to another one of Isabella and Ferdinand's daughters. The fifth child of their marriage, Catherine, married Arthur, Prince of Wales, before marrying King Henry VIII of Great Britain. She is known to history as Catherine of Aragon.

Although these alliances were important, Joanna played an important role in the destiny of Spain. In 1504, Isabella died, and the throne went to Joanna, the eldest surviving child of Isabella and Ferdinand. However, Ferdinand was not happy with this arrangement, and a brief civil war sprung up. In 1506, Ferdinand recognized Joanna and her husband, the Habsburg Philip, as the new monarchs. Philip died the same year, and due to Joanna's mental deficiencies, Ferdinand again took over, although Joanna still ruled in name. When he passed in 1516, Joanna's son, Charles, inherited the throne, ruling alongside his mother until she passed in 1555. Charles I became Charles V of the Holy Roman Empire in 1519.

In 1556, Charles I abdicated his throne and gave the monarchy of Spain to his son, Philip II. He awarded the Holy Roman Empire to his brother, Ferdinand I.

The Dutch

William the Silent had been dispatched from Spain as governor of the Spanish Netherlands. William, like his populace, was opposed to the persecution that occurred when Calvinism, a Protestant sect, arose in the 16th century and spread across Europe. The coming of this and other non-Catholic religions upset the Catholic monopoly on religions. Because of the persecutions of Calvinists and the heavy-handed control of Habsburg Spain over the Netherlands, the populace rebelled. Seventeen Dutch provinces demanded their independence. This was the start of the Eighty Years' War, also known as the Dutch War of Independence. William led the rebels in the northern provinces, but Philip II scored some successes.

In 1581, William ejected the Habsburg troops and established their own territory in the northern Netherlands called the Dutch Republic. The fight for their independence continued against the backdrop of other European conflicts over religion and economy—odd bedfellows indeed. A ten-year-truce with the Dutch was ironed out in 1588.

Anglo-Spanish War (1585–1604)

In 1584, Philip II of Spain signed the secret Treaty of Joinville with the French Catholic League, stating that it was his intention to eradicate Protestantism. Queen Elizabeth I of England believed this treaty meant a Catholic alliance would be formed. If France successfully invaded England, Elizabeth would be dethroned, and her Catholic cousin, Mary, Queen of Scotland, who had a right to the throne, would more than likely take her place and kill her. In February of 1587, Elizabeth had her cousin executed. The Catholics in Europe were furious. Mary's claim on the English throne was passed onto Philip of Spain. Philip was intent on placing a Catholic monarch on the English throne, and in retaliation for Elizabeth's execution of Mary, he planned to invade England.

However, before he could set out on the warpath, Sir Francis Drake burned thirty-seven Spanish ships at Cádiz, forcing Philip to delay the invasion. Philip knew he would get papal support, as the Protestant Queen Elizabeth had already been excommunicated by Pope Pius V for heresy. Pope Sixtus V granted his support and permitted Philip to collect taxes for the battle. Philip then assembled about 130 ships, which carried around 18,000 sailors and 8,000 soldiers.

On May 8th, 1588, the Spanish Armada sailed for the Netherlands to pick up some additional troops. When the Armada sailed through the English Channel, the English navy was waiting. Sir Francis Drake planned on engaging the Spanish from Plymouth to Portland and then at the Solent. The Spanish Armada withdrew and anchored off the coast of

Calais in France in a crescent formation. It was hit at night by English fireships. The Spanish Armada scattered, then reformed.

Things were not going well for the Spanish, and it would continue to get worse. The Spanish Armada was delayed because of bad weather at the Bay of Biscay. Four of their ships were forced to turn back, and some had to be put in for repair, leaving the Spanish with just 124 ships. In mid-July, the Spanish spotted the English at Plymouth Harbor, where it was trapped by the incoming tide. Philip II forbade the Spanish to engage, and they instead sailed toward the Isle of Wight. When the tide came in, though, Charles Howard and Francis Drake sent out fifty-five ships to confront the Spanish. On July 20th, they went upwind of the Armada and engaged the Spanish fleet near the Eddystone Rocks off the coast of Plymouth. The Armada went into their familiar crescent-shaped pattern, while the English ships were broken up into two divisions. Drake went to the north in the *Revenge*, and Howard took the *Ark Royal* south with most of the fleet. They then hit the Armada with cannon fire. By the end of the day, there was no clear winner, although the Spanish lost two ships when they crashed into each other. At night, Drake looted the deserted Spanish ships, capturing gold and gunpowder. Due to this move, the English ships became disarrayed and scattered.

Eventually, the English regrouped, and they caught up with the Spanish on July 23rd off the coast of Portland. The Spanish were foiled by the maneuverability of the English fleet, and the Armada sought out the Solent, which was a protected strait. Alonso Pérez de Guzmán, Duke of Medina Sidonia, ordered the Armada back out onto the open sea to avoid being foundered upon the shallow shoals. The arrival of Alexander Farnese, Duke of Parma, and his reinforcement fleet had been delayed. Therefore, the Armada headed back to Calais.

The Defeat of the Spanish Armada

On July 27th, the Armada was anchored at Calais in their typical crescent formation. Word finally came that Parma's forces had been very ill and wasn't yet equipped for transport. The estimate was that it would take him six more days.

Medina Sidonia waited at Dunkirk but was blockaded by a Dutch fleet, who were allied with the English. Parma sent word that he wanted some ships to push away the Dutch, but Medina wouldn't send them, thinking he might need them himself. The difficulty was the fact that they had deep keels that needed deep-water ports to anchor. Another problem facing the Armada was the fact that Parma's army from Flanders needed barges to cross the English Channel. Of course, that was protected by the Dutch. In planning the invasion, the Spanish had overlooked that possibility.

On July 28th, the English sent out eight fireships, sacrificing some of their own ships in the process. They cast them downwind toward the Armada. Two were intercepted in time, but two others moved forward. The Armada scattered to avoid the conflagration.

The Battle of Gravelines

Now that the Armada's formation had been broken up, the English headed in for a confrontation. The two fleets headed for the port of Gravelines. Medina Sidonia had to stay in open waters because of his deep keel ships. The English, however, had no such disadvantage and moved in closer.

Drake and his seamen fired off a few shots from their guns to provoke the Spanish. They broadsided the Spanish with gunfire aimed below the waterline. Many Spanish gunners lost their lives, so the guns had to be handled by the foot soldiers, who didn't know how to use them. As the English and Spanish neared each other, the crews exchanged musket fire. However, after hours, the English were running out of ammunition, and they pulled back. Five Spanish ships had been lost, and many were greatly damaged.

The Fate of the Armada off Ireland

In September 1588, the Spanish Armada headed toward the west coast of Ireland, hopeful to use the natural protection of that island before going south to return home. After fumbling around in the winds, some ships made landfall in the Irish province of Munster. Many ships were sighted off the coast of County Clare along the southwestern coast. Two were wrecked there, including the *San Esteban*. The *San Marcos*, a ship from Portugal, was damaged on a small island nearby. All who survived were executed by Boetius MacClancy, who was the sheriff there. At that time, much of Ireland was occupied by the British.

At the Blasket Islands, Juan Martínez de Recalde, who had some experience sailing near Ireland, sighted Mount Brandon in an area peppered with reeds. He navigated around those carefully and arrived at a protected area, where he dropped anchor into sandy soil. Recalde sent a scouting party inland, but all eight members of the group were captured.

Recalde then sailed to A Coruña, Galicia, Spain. He had been wounded in his battles and contracted a fever. Recalde died there a few days later.

The *Nuestra Senora del Socorro,* a sloop that had been a part of the Armada, anchored near the coast of County Kerry. The sheriff was right there, waiting for the ship to arrive. All twenty-four seamen were taken to Tralee Castle and hanged.

In Donegal, *La Trinidad Valencera* was taking on water. The sailors paid some local Irishmen for a small boat, and all were brought ashore. Unfortunately, they were met by an English cavalry force under Richard and Henry Hovenden and were taken into custody. The Spanish laid down their arms, and the noblemen and officers were separated from the crew. Some of the members of the crew were massacred, but about 150 managed to escape and fled through the bogs. Some reached the house of the bishop of Derry, and he had them brought to Scotland. Thirty officers and nobles were sent to London, where they were held for ransom.

As one can tell, the weather practically decimated the Spanish Armada. Numerous Spanish ships arrived on the Irish coastlines, many of them damaged. Between seventeen and twenty-four ships from the Armada were lost along the Irish coasts. That was one-third of the entire Armada. The estimate of Spanish deaths in Ireland was about 6,000 men.

After the defeat of the Spanish Armada, England sent its own fleet against the Iberian Peninsula. It suffered similar losses. The result of the Anglo-Spanish War was described as being "status quo ante bellum," meaning "The situation as it existed before the war."

The Spanish Inquisition: "The Bringer of Darkness"

In the 16th century, Spain reverted again into an era of purification under the Inquisition. An overzealous cleric by the name of Diego Rodríguez Lucero, also called the "Bringer of Darkness," became the most prominent and active inquisitor. Regardless of whether possible suspects were *conversos*, noblemen, non-Catholic Christians, or peasants, no one was spared investigation once attention was drawn to their name.

Lucero used the powers given to him by the office of the Inquisition to examine religious differences. He targeted Julian Trigueros and sentenced him to burn at the stake. The offense? Lucero wanted Trigueros's wife, so he concocted charges and had the unfortunate man burned at the stake! When Lucero wanted a mistress, he would burn her one living parent and her husband to stop their complaints. When his cruelty came to light in 1506, his prisoners were released. Lucero was arrested, but he, too, was soon released, much to the consternation of many.

New inquisitors were appointed, and they continued to go after converts to the Catholic faith. In 1620, William Lithgow, a Scottish traveler, was suspected of being a spy. Examination of his books revealed that he had placed notes within his Bible criticizing Catholic teachings. Calvinism was the latest Protestant sect that had arisen at that time, and Lithgow was accused of being a Calvinist; in other words, a "heretic."

The Spanish Inquisition didn't deal with many cases in regards to Protestants, as there weren't very many in Spain. The most heavily persecuted sect of Protestants were Lutherans, with some of the more prominent trials taking place in the mid-1550s. One way in which inquisitors got confessions from non-conforming Catholics was through torture. Lithgow was not only tortured, but he was also starved. In the end, he was sentenced to be burned to death. Fortunately, the governor of Málaga intervened, and Lithgow was released, but he sustained permanent damage to his arm.

Aside from eliminating heresy, the Inquisition became a convenient way to punish people for other crimes, mostly ones of a sexual nature. In Aragon, cases of sodomy could be handled by the court of the Inquisition. Normally, sodomy was considered a secular crime, but the Inquisition treated it like a capital offense and issued the death penalty.

The Golden Age of Spain (c. 1580–1680)

Under the Habsburgs, art and literature flourished. Diego Velázquez was a famous painter who followed the heavily ornamental style of the Baroque period. He was a court painter and influenced many who followed in his footsteps.

Doménikos Theotokópoulos, better known as El Greco, was a Greek immigrant who settled in Spain. He brought with him the styles of the Italian Renaissance.

El Greco's View of Toledo painted 1596–1600

Francisco de Zurbarán painted the religious themes that were so prevalent at the time. Among his themes, which were instructive, were renderings of St. Francis of Assisi; Mary, the mother of Jesus Christ; and the crucifixion.

Bartolomé Esteban Murillo studied at the art school in Seville. His paintings were very realistic and similar to that of the Flemish school. His work appealed to the clergy and the bourgeoisie. Religious art was prominent in his repertoire, and he painted pictures that were displayed in the Seville Cathedral. Later, he founded the Academy of Art in Madrid.

Some of the world's greatest composers came from Spain, such as Tomás Luis de Victoria and Luis de Milán. When it came to literature, one of Spain's most famous works came from Miguel de Cervantes. He wrote *Don Quixote de la Mancha*, which is thought to be the world's first modern novel. Lope de Vega, a playwright, wrote about 1,000 plays, of which over 400 survive today.

The Decline of the Habsburgs

In 1598, Philip II died, and he was succeeded by his son, who became Philip III. In 1618, Spain became involved in a massive European conflict known as the Thirty Years' War. Philip III died in 1621 and was succeeded by Philip IV. He was a weak ruler, and the country was commandeered by Gaspar de Guzmán, also known simply as the Count-Duke of Olivares, who essentially took over foreign affairs. Olivares was adamant about taking back the Dutch Republic, which the Spanish had reluctantly recognized as a political entity in 1609. The Dutch efforts for independence in the Eighty Years' War wouldn't end until 1648. Since Spain had to finance the war efforts in both the Eighty Years' War and the Thirty Years' War, the economy of Spain declined.

In 1647, the Great Plague of Seville broke out, robbing Seville of 25 percent of its population. Tax collection declined, as the people who survived weren't able to make up the deficit in the country's treasury.

The Reapers' War (1640-1659)

France was threatened by the Habsburg presence on either side of its empire: Spain on its west and the Holy Roman Empire on its east. This war resembled a religious war, although power and territory were basically at the heart of the matter.

In the 1630s, Spain increased taxes in order to pay for its many wars. Portugal and Catalonia rebelled when Cardinal Richelieu, who had a hidden agenda, urged them to do so. In 1641, the Catalans declared that they were a republic. Spain sent in 26,000 troops to defeat them. On its way to Barcelona, the Spanish army took some cities and executed hundreds of prisoners. On January 23rd, 1641, at Martorell, the rebels of the Catalan Republic were defeated. Three days later, the Catalans scored a victory against the Spanish army at Montjuïc.

However, the rebellion was uncontrollable in some areas, as it started to focus on the Catalan nobility. This divided the Catalans, with some fighting for its independence and some fighting against the ruling classes. Once that occurred, the French were able to take control of the County of Rousillon and the northern area of County Cerdagne. The Spanish border was now pulled back farther into the Pyrenees.

According to the Peace of Westphalia, which ended the Thirty Years' War in 1648, Catholics and Protestants were seen as equals before the law. The independence of the Dutch Republic remained in place, and it was agreed that they were free to practice religious tolerance.

Charles II ascended to the Habsburg throne in Spain in 1665. Historian John Langdon-Davies said of him, "Of no man is it more true to say that in his beginning was his end; from the day of his birth, they were waiting for his death." It was an unkind reference to Charles's physical disabilities and unhealthy life. However, it was an omen that shadowed him, as he was the last of the Habsburgs in Spain. He died childless in November 1700. However, he did have a will and named Philip, Duke of Anjou and the grandson of the French king, as his successor to the Spanish crown. Philip was the son of Charles II's half-sister, so there was a familial relationship between the two. Philip, who came from the House of Bourbon, became Philip V of Spain. The Bourbons originated in the 13th century in France and gave rise to monarchs who held thrones in Spain, Sicily, Naples, and Parma.

However, there was a problem with having Philip as the successor. Philip V was already King Louis XIV's heir. This meant that he would be entitled to the French throne in addition to the Spanish one. This would have created an alliance so powerful that many other European countries would be adversely affected. There would be no balance of power. Britain, the Holy Roman Empire, Savoy, the Dutch Republic, and those who backed the Habsburgs in Spain declared war on France and Bourbon Spain in 1701. Later on, other nations became involved, such as Portugal and Prussia.

The War of the Spanish Succession

France and Britain were perennial enemies, especially when Britain became a Protestant country. France, under Louis XIV, was Catholic. Spain, too, had been united under the Catholic Monarchs, Ferdinand II and Isabella I. The preservation of the British economy was also an issue, so its access to the Mediterranean was essential. In 1701, there were two political factions in the country: the Tories and the Whigs. The Tories felt that the Royal Navy was essential in protecting economic interests and fostering trade. The Whigs, on the other hand, felt that they couldn't depend upon the navy alone and needed more alliances to keep France in check. The Whigs won, and soon the whole country felt that the succession crisis in Spain should be resolved in order to bring about peace in Europe.

The Dutch Republic had been trying to maintain itself amongst the growing powers that surrounded them. It felt threatened by the control of Spain, which had possession of the Spanish Netherlands to their south.

They wanted to maintain a number of barrier fortresses to assure the protection of their southern border.

The Duchy of Savoy, which entered the war in 1703, was wedged between France and the Duchy of Milan, which was controlled by Spain. Savoy had historical ties to France, so it was initially allied with France. However, its duke, Victor Amadeus II, was looking to diminish French power in Savoy, especially because England was becoming stronger after it obtained the command of the Mediterranean trade. So, by 1703, Savoy had switched sides.

The Duchy of Austria, to the northeast of the Italian Peninsula, was a part of the Holy Roman Empire during this time. The Holy Roman Empire was a confederation of multi-ethnic countries, which included Germany and northern Italy. In Italy, Spain ruled the Duchies of Milan and Mantua in the north. Austria was concerned about the integrity of those duchies, as it wanted to protect its southern borders.

Louis XIV of France needed an alliance with Spain and Bavaria in southeast Germany to secure its borders with the Holy Roman Empire. He also wanted to decrease the power of the Duchy of Austria, as its downfall would more than likely spell the end for the Holy Roman Empire. Primarily, though, Louis craved the wealth that could come from the New World.

Spain was still in an economic decline and depended upon the wealthy nobles of Castile for financial support. It also relied upon its trade with the New World to supplement its financial needs.

The Battle of Luzzara

At the Battle of Luzzara in 1702, Prince Eugene led the troops for the Holy Roman Empire. On the opposing side was Vendôme, the French general, Philip V of Spain, Victor Amadeus of Savoy, and Duke Ferdinando Gonzaga of Mantua. Vendôme and his allies suffered as many as 4,000 casualties, while the opposition incurred just 2,000. It was a bloody battle, according to historical documents, but the French offensive was halted. For an entire month, the two armies just stared at each other in this area of the Po Valley in northern Italy's Duchy of Mantua. Even though Vendôme lost more men than his enemies, the outcome of the battle has been considered a draw by military experts.

The Siege of Turin

In 1706, France occupied most of Savoy; all that was really left to conquer was Turin, its capital. In April, Vendôme won a major victory in Lombardy, so everyone was surprised when he was recalled to France and replaced by Philippe II, Duke of Orléans. The siege of Turin began in early June, but unfortunately, Philippe wasn't a very competent fighter. Prince Eugene of the Holy Roman Empire outwitted him by joining up with Victor Amadeus. They attacked the French just south of Turin and lifted the siege. By virtue of the Convention of Milan, which ended the war in northern Italy, Holy Roman Emperor Joseph I was forced to grant the French troops in Lombardy passage into southern France. The Allies then confiscated the Spanish Kingdom of Naples, a Bourbon-controlled territory.

The Battle of Ramillies

In late May 1706, at the village of Ramillies in the Spanish Netherlands, King Louis XIV's French army, led by the duke of Villeroi, experienced a humiliating defeat. Afterward, Villeroi never again received an important command, sadly remarking, "I cannot foresee a happy day in my life save only that of my death."

The Battle of Saragossa

In August 1710, General James Stanhope led the center force of British, Portuguese, and Austrian troops. He attacked Philip V's left wing. Initially, the Spanish prevailed, but the assault left a gap in the Spanish line, and Stanhope charged in. The Spanish fought back with ferocity, but the Allies stood firm, and the Spanish were finally pushed back. After less than three hours of brutal fighting, Stanhope's forces were able to seize their enemy's cannons. In the end, about 6,000 Spanish soldiers were wounded or slaughtered. Another 7,000 were taken as prisoners.

The Peace of Utrecht

In 1713, at the city of Utrecht in the Dutch Republic, the Peace of Utrecht was drawn up. It was the outcome of a number of ongoing negotiations between France and Spain and the Allied countries in Europe. The treaty ensured territorial changes would take place that would benefit all the parties. The nations of Europe needed to be assured the balance of power would not tip into anyone's favor. Below are some of the concessions made by the participating countries:

Philip V would be allowed to be the king of Spain, but he and his successors couldn't claim the French throne; likewise, the French Bourbons couldn't claim the Spanish throne.

Spain would cede the Spanish Netherlands and Milan to Austria, forming the Austrian Netherlands.

The Dutch Republic would be allowed to build and maintain its barrier fortresses that had been lost earlier in the war.

Great Britain was awarded Gibraltar and Minorca in the western Mediterranean.

Victor Amadeus II was recognized as the king of Sicily.

Chapter 8 – Bourbon Spain

The War of the Quadruple Alliance

Philip V and his wife, Elizabeth of Parma, wanted Spain's former holdings restored. Sicily and Sardinia were their first targets. Once they realized Spain's intentions, Britain, France, and the Dutch Republic formed what was called the "Triple Alliance." They wanted to enforce the terms of the Treaty of Utrecht and were willing to engage in war if need be.

In 1717, Spain sent out a fleet across the Mediterranean to Sardinia. It was an ideal time to attack because Austria was involved in a war with the Ottoman Empire. The Sardinians were discontented with their domination by Austria, so it seemed as if they would be open to having Spain rule over them. By November, Spain had control of Sardinia, obtaining it with relative ease. Diplomatic attempts to resolve this crisis failed, so, in June of 1718, Britain sent a naval force into the western Mediterranean.

In July 1718, Spain sent over 30,000 troops to Sicily. Soon after this, Austria, which had ended its war with the Ottoman Empire, decided to join up with the Triple Alliance, making it the "Quadruple Alliance."

The Spanish took Palermo on July 7th. Marquess of Lede, who worked for Spain, placed a siege upon Messina, and the duke of Montemar conquered the rest of the island. In the fall, the Austrians arrived to lift the siege of Messina. They were defeated, though, at the First Battle of Milazzo in October.

In 1719, Philippe II, Duke of Orléans, had his French army invade the Basque districts in Spain. They were forced back because of losses due to disease. In Sicily, the Austrians started a campaign but were defeated at the Battle of Francavilla in June 1719. However, the tides would turn in their favor. The British fleet flew into action and cut off Spain from its homeland. This allowed the Quadruple Alliance to score a victory in the Second Battle of Milazzo. They took Messina back in October and then besieged Palermo.

This war even took place in the New World. In May 1719, the French captured the Spanish settlement of Pensacola, Florida. The Spanish took it back later, but it then fell into French hands again. Spain even tried to take Nassau from the British, but although they managed to make off with some riches, they were unable to conquer the British settlement.

The Treaty of Hague

By virtue of the Treaty of the Hague, which was signed in 1720, Philip V confirmed the terms of the Treaty of Utrecht, which stated he had no claim to the French throne or the former Spanish possessions in Italy. Philip V's son, Charles, was seen as the heir to the Duchies of Parma, Tuscany, and Piacenza. Savoy and Austria also swapped Sicily for Sardinia.

Philip's Temporary Abdication

On January 14th, 1724, Philip V abdicated the throne to his seventeen-year-old son, Louis. Some historians believe he was becoming mentally unstable. Others indicate that the French were prone to hereditary illnesses and that Philip wanted to ensure the succession went smoothly in case of his sudden death. His abdication actually occurred just after the death of Philippe II, Duke of Orléans, who was the regent for King Louis XV of France. Yet another theory suggests that this abdication might have made it possible for him to avoid the terms of the Treaty of Utrecht, which forbade the union of the French and Spanish crowns until the death of the last Bourbon male.

However, Philip's son died a little over seven months later to smallpox. Since Louis had no children, and Philip's younger son wasn't of age, Philip took back his throne. His attention moved to regaining some of the territories Spain had lost and to reducing threats from its enemies, such as Austria. He allied with Louis XV, the French Bourbon king, and sent forces into central Europe to fight in two wars: the War of the Polish Succession and the War of the Austrian Succession. These wars allowed Spain to make some territorial gains; it took Naples and Sicily from Austria, as well as Oran, Algeria, from the Ottoman Empire.

Death of Philip V

Philip V was clinically depressed during most of his reign, and as he grew older, they only became worse. In 1746, he died. His son, Ferdinand VI, became the next king and was thrown into the closing years of the War of the Austrian Succession.

Ferdinand VI

Philip V had bankrupted the country. His administration spent a lot of money financing its many wars and well-paid family retainers. Ferdinand worked with the Marquis of Ensenada to rescue Spain from the financial tailspin it was in. His reforms were unpopular and were rejected by the powerful nobility. However, the bank Giro Real designed a system whereby private and public funds were put into the royal treasury.

Commerce with the Americas was stimulated when Ferdinand and his advisor broke the monopoly on trade by the companies in the Indies.

Like his father, Ferdinand had a mental illness. In 1758, he was so incapacitated that he was sent to a castle in a municipality of Madrid known as Villaviciosa de Odón. Although his state was described as "prostration," a state of physical and emotional exhaustion, the symptoms that were described resemble that of severe clinical depression and what is called "frontal lobe syndrome," an epileptic condition. Ferdinand was there for a full year—from 1758 to 1759—and it was called "the year without a king." Ferdinand died on August 10th, 1759.

Charles III

Ferdinand had no children, so he was succeeded by Charles III, his half-brother. Charles practiced "enlightened absolutism," meaning he adopted the principles of the Enlightenment, which emphasized rationality. Those principles tended to allow for religious tolerance, the freedom of the press, the freedom of speech, and the freedom to own personal property. Charles attempted to try to unite Spain into a "nation-state" rather than a collection of kingdoms.

The Third Pacte de Famille

The "Family Compact," or "Pacte de Famille," was an alliance between Bourbon France and Bourbon Spain. The first pact followed the War of the Spanish Succession, which forbade the thrones of France and Spain to unite. The second pact was signed in the midst of the War of Austrian Succession. And in 1761, the third pact was formulated.

France was fighting the Seven Years' War against Britain and other countries. Portugal had declared neutrality but was having trouble maintaining that stance because of minor incidents between Britain and France. For example, on one occasion, Portugal had permitted Britain to prevent a French warship from unloading in one of its harbors. Portugal and England had an alliance since the 14th century (the Anglo-Portuguese Alliance), and Portugal had been honoring that agreement. France wanted Portugal to break that neutrality and close its ports to British ships.

Spain had also declared neutrality, but France wanted Spanish assistance in fighting against Britain and breaking Portugal's alliance with them. Because both the French and Spanish kings were Bourbons, France expected Spain to join the war effort. With this pact, Charles III signaled his loyalty to France and entered the war.

Spain in the Seven Years' War: European Theater

In late 1761, Spain placed an embargo on British goods. Britain then declared war in early 1762, kicking off the Anglo-Spanish War, which was a part of the larger Seven Years' War. In late April, Spain entered Portugal and announced that they came to free the Portuguese people from the "heavy shackles of England, the tyrant of the seas."

The First Invasion of Portugal

In the following month, the Marquis of Sarria led a force of 22,000 men and invaded Portugal. Portugal soon declared war on Spain and France. The Spanish believed this show of power would make Portugal quickly submit, but it didn't work. The Spanish were not well supplied, so they forced requisitions on the population, instigating a revolt that spread nationwide. The Spanish incurred heavy losses, mostly from disease and starvation. The British press reported that Spain retaliated for their failure by committing "unheard of barbarities among the small villages; robbing and murdering the inhabitants; and setting fire to their crops."

The Spanish had been defeated by the peasants and disease instead of a professional standing army. But they would soon try their hand again at taking over Portugal.

The Second Invasion of Portugal

In September 1762, two Spanish corps were joined by a French army, placing the number of men to 30,000 Spaniards and 12,000 French. The Portuguese-British troops consisted of 7,000 to 8,000 Portuguese soldiers and a little over 7,000 British. A British observer described the Portuguese as the most "wretched troops" he had ever seen.

The Franco-Spanish forces entered Beria province, occupied several fortresses, and captured the garrison at Almeida. Although it seems like this would be a great victory, it wasn't in the long run. The Spanish were not well equipped to hold onto a fort, and the areas they took over were not readily accessible by roads. In addition to this, another revolt broke out, and disease was rampant among the soldiers.

The Spanish went on the offensive toward the town of Abrantes. Commander Lippe was anticipating this move, and he sent men to occupy the strategic positions around the nearby Tagus River. The Spanish could either turn around and head home or go through the mountains for Lisbon. Since turning around would be seen as cowardly and since Lisbon was the ultimate goal, the Spanish-Franco forces pushed onward. The Spanish forces attempted to take Abrantes but failed. The Portuguese soldiers and peasant population had virtually abandoned Beria province, taking everything edible with them and burning their fields as they left. There was nothing for the Spanish to use, and there was nowhere they could go except backward. In his memoirs, Commander Lippe wrote, "they were reduced to a forced inaction while the difficulties of subsistence, desertion and disease decimated them." By October of 1762, it was clear that the second Franco-Spanish offensive was a failure.

The Third Invasion of Portugal

During the winter, the Spanish commander, Pedro Pablo Abarca, Count of Aranda, received intelligence from British Brigadier General

Charles Rainsford, who told the count that the province of Alentejo would be in a weak condition. However, what he didn't know was that Lippe of the Portuguese army was taking precautions in the meantime. He saw to it that Alentejo's forts near the border (Elvas, Ouguela, Marvão, Alegrete, Arronches, and Campo Maior) were strengthened.

When the Spanish attempted to take Marvão, the terrified population begged the commanding officer to surrender. However, he encouraged them, indicating that they could overcome the enemy. And he was right. At Ouguela, which was just a small fortress, the Portuguese routed the Spanish. The assault on Campo Maior also failed because the Spanish lacked backup.

Realizing they had lost, the Franco-Spanish army commander, the Count of Aranda, sent Major General Antonio María Bucarelli to the Anglo-Portuguese headquarters at Monforte with a peace proposal. It was signed in December 1763.

Spain in the Seven Years' War: Other Theaters

While Spain was invading Portugal, the British were invading Spanish colonial holdings in the Americas and the Pacific.

The Captured Spanish Fleet at Havana, Cuba
https://commons.wikimedia.org/wiki/File:Dominic_Serres_the_Elder_-_The_Captured_Spanish_Fleet_at_Havana,_August-September_1762.jpg

Cuba was a Spanish colony, and the British mounted a successful attack on the fortification of Morro Castle and captured the Spanish fleet at the naval base at Havana, its major port, in the summer of 1762. This weakened the Spanish presence in the Caribbean and gave Britain greater security for its colonies in North America.

The British Occupation of Manila, Philippines

In September of 1762, Admiral Samuel Cornish of the Royal Navy sent a three-pronged force to land at Manila Bay in the Philippines, which was another Spanish colony. The fortifications at Manila were incomplete and hence not formidable. A storm blew in, though, and the British storeship was grounded, and communications were cut off. About 1,000 native Pampangos tried to defend the harbor but were forced to withdraw when 300 of them were killed. Governor-General Archbishop Manuel Rojo del Rio y Vieyra soon surrendered Manila and the neighboring fort of Cavite to the British, as he wished to prevent more deaths. The English occupied Manila until 1763.

The Treaty of Paris, 1763

The Treaty of Paris ended the Seven Years' War. Spain and France restored all their conquered territories to Britain and Portugal, and Britain returned Havana and Manila to Spain.

The Treaty of Paris is often thought to be when France gave Louisiana to Spain. However, this had already happened in the secret Treaty of Fontainebleau, which was signed in 1762. However, the treaty wasn't officially announced until 1764. In the Treaty of Paris, Britain was given the eastern side of the Mississippi, while France retained the important port of New Orleans. Even though the territory belonged to the Spanish, they had no objection to this, as they knew they still controlled western Louisiana.

Chapter 9 – War of the Third Coalition, 1803–1806

Napoleon Bonaparte declared himself the emperor of France in 1804. In 1805, Spain and France were allies. Napoleon had designs upon conquering Great Britain. Toward that end, France sent out Admiral Pierre Villeneuve, who oversaw a combined fleet of thirty-three French and Spanish ships. The fleet set sail from the Spanish port of Cádiz in southern Spain. The Franco-Spanish forces encountered Admiral Lord Horatio Nelson of Britain off Cape Trafalgar. Nelson was a formidable enemy and an expert at naval warfare. He organized his fleet and rammed it straight into the Franco-Spanish lines. Villeneuve and his seamen weren't well organized, but they fought back valiantly. Nelson's lead warship, the HMS *Victory*, was badly damaged by the thundering cannons. Despite its damage, the *Victory* was able to engage French vessels, namely the *Redoutable* and the *Bucentaure*. At one point, the *Victory*'s mast locked with up with the *Redoutable*'s mast, and the French attempted to board. A shot fired out from the deck of the *Redoutable*, and Nelson was struck. Just as the French attempted to board the HMS *Victory*, another British ship fired on the French. Many sailors fell, and Captain Jean Lucas surrendered after more British ships attacked.

More and more English ships joined the fray, attacking the center of the Franco-Spanish line of vessels, and the combined fleet was overwhelmed. The British confiscated twenty-two of the French ships. The *Redoutable* was not one of them, as it sank in the melee. Only ten ships returned to Cádiz. Although Lord Nelson died, the British won the battle.

The Spanish military garrison dispatched rescue parties along the southern Spanish coast. Wreckage could be seen everywhere at sea. The Spanish Navy was practically obliterated. What's more, the Spanish military wasn't prepared to deal with armed conflicts in the early 19th century. Unfortunately for them, this was when Napoleon struck.

Conflicts with Portugal

In 1807, Napoleon Bonaparte and Spain invaded Portugal. His military force under Jean-Andoche Junot marched through Spain to Lisbon. John, the prince regent of Portugal, along with some of the nobility, escaped to Brazil in South America. This allowed the French and their Spanish allies to more easily occupy Portugal. The Spanish king, Charles IV, made no contribution to these efforts, as he was being silenced by the overwhelming power of his prime minister, Manuel Godoy, who'd been hired by his parents. Godoy created a secret agreement in which France planned to carve up Portugal into three entities, one of which would be awarded to Godoy.

In 1808, the French crossed the Pyrenees and entered northern Spain, taking over Navarre, Catalonia, and the important citadels of Pamplona and Barcelona. Since they were allies of Napoleon, the Spanish demanded an explanation but received nothing to their satisfaction. Therefore, Spain withdrew from Portugal. According to historians, Napoleon had no intention of abiding by the agreement he made with Godoy; he simply wanted to take over Portugal, which had been allied with Britain.

Napoleon appointed Joachim Murat as the head of all the French troops in Spain. The Spanish citizens, riled up by King Charles's son's rumors that Godoy had sold Spain to France, rose up, demanding King Charles IV to abdicate. To save Godoy's life, Charles did just that. The throne was then thrust upon Charles's son, Ferdinand VII, which was exactly what he wanted. When Ferdinand sought Napoleon's confirmation of his accession, the emperor summoned both Charles and Ferdinand to France. He had both of them abdicate before him and then pressured the Spanish governmental authority, the junta, into appointing Joseph Bonaparte, Napoleon's brother, as the new king of Spain.

Spain under Joseph Bonaparte

The Spanish government accepted Joseph Bonaparte as the new king, but the population denounced the attitude of the nobility. The people of Madrid rebelled, and the French retaliated by shooting hundreds of civilians.

The Catalans defeated the French outside of Barcelona. When the French tried to capture the city of Girona, they were forced to retreat. This was the typical pattern for the Peninsular War. Although the French won a few battles, overall, they were unsuccessful at easily putting down the rebels.

Despite this fighting, Madrid was still under French control, and Joseph Bonaparte entered Madrid in triumph and was crowned the king of Spain on July 25th, 1808.

The foreign secretary of England, George Canning, offered peaceful relations to Spain in the summer of 1808, as both countries were under constant threat from Napoleon Bonaparte's imperialistic ambitions. Canning declared, "No longer remember that war has existed between Spain and Great Britain. Every nation which resists the exorbitant power of France becomes immediately, and whatever may have been its previous relations with us, the natural ally of Great Britain." Spain graciously accepted.

Off the coast of Cádiz, French ships were seized by Spain. General Pierre Dupont de L'Etang was marching toward Córdoba when this happened, but he fell back to a safer location. The Spanish junta combined their forces and moved to attack Dupont. Once Dupont saw the size of the Spanish forces, he pulled back and called for reinforcements. While waiting, the Spanish descended upon him at Bailén. Dupont tried to break up the Spanish but failed. About 3,000 French were killed or wounded, while the Spanish had around 1,000 casualties. Seventeen thousand French were dragged away as prisoners. It was a disaster for France. Joseph Bonaparte abandoned Madrid for his own safety and hid with some supporters in Castile. The Spanish troops rapidly reoccupied it and were able to keep the French troops penned up below the Ebro River.

The Spanish general, Xavier de Castanos, said this about the victory over the French army: "This army, so superior to ours, has not only been beaten and routed, but has been constrained to lay down its arms, and give up its artillery, and has suffered the lowest military degradation."

The Peninsular War: Second Phase

Britain started their aid to the Iberian Peninsula by sending General Arthur Wellesley, 1ˢᵗ Duke of Wellington, into Portugal. He repelled the French and attacked Commander Henri François Delaborde at Roliça and then destroyed Jean-Andoche Junot's army at Vimeiro at the end of August 1808.

Napoleon was astonished at his defeats and had his tremendous army of nearly 300,000 men attack Burgos, Tudela, Somosierra, and Espinosa. He forced Madrid to surrender in early December and restored his brother to the throne.

In 1809, Napoleon's troops conquered the province of León and defeated the British forces. Discipline broke down among the British forces, which allowed Corunna, in the province of Galicia, to be taken by the French. General John Moore of Great Britain lost his life there.

The Spanish people insisted that the junta reestablish itself. It was set up in January in Cádiz, and plans were made to recapture Madrid and the territories still under French control. The Duke del Parque, Juan Carlos de Aréizaga, and the Duke of Albuquerque sent out their troops. Del Parque reoccupied Salamanca but was forced to abandon it. Aréizaga lost to the French at Ocaña, and Albuquerque had to abandon his drive near Talavera.

French troops then poured into southern Spain and captured town after town. Spain went into a crisis over this, and in 1810, the junta required all men over twenty-five to be drafted. They even insisted that the Spanish colonists in South America were also subject to the draft. Because the Spanish in the American colonies considered this a European war, they deeply resented that.

Spain never missed a chance to harass the French troops inside Spain with hit-and-run guerilla attacks. In addition to the loss of lives, the French started to find it difficult to keep their supply lines active. Napoleon, who thought that Spain would be an easy conquest, wryly remarked at one point that these conflicts were the "Spanish ulcer."

Joseph Bonaparte

Joseph Bonaparte was a reluctant Spanish king. He was also the king of Naples, which he preferred over Spain because he was very popular there. In Spain, he was greeted with revolts and mobs. Even though he didn't have a drinking problem, people called him "Pepe Botella," meaning "Joe Bottle," in order to disparage his reputation.

Spanish cartoon depicting "Joe Bottle."

During the Peninsular War, Joseph Bonaparte spent much of his time in northern Spain, which was relatively quiet. The French military always checked with Joseph Bonaparte before making any major moves.

In March of 1811, the French forces were down to between 20,000 and 15,000 men. The British, under Lieutenant General Thomas Graham, and the Spanish, under General Manuel La Peña, defeated two French divisions at Barrosa on the Atlantic coast. Between November 3rd, 1811, and January 9th, 1812, Louis Gabriel Suchet moved down to Valencia, took it, and secured a castle at Saguntum.

Badajoz was a hotly contested city during the Peninsular War. Between March and April of 1812, Arthur Wellesley had the opportunity to recapture Badajoz. It was, by far, one of the bloodiest battles of the war, but Wellesley was successful. He pushed inward, fighting a decisive battle at Salamanca in June. After this battle, Joseph fled Madrid. It didn't help that Napoleon pulled troops out of France in 1812 to fight in his disastrous campaign against Russia.

The Spanish and British continued to win battle after battle, pushing Joseph back. On June 21st, 1813, King Joseph led his troops at the Battle of Vitoria. This was yet another defeat for the French, and Joseph abdicated on December 11th, 1813.

The war continued on, but France could never truly recover from its losses, although it did win some victories. In April 1814, Napoleon and the Allies agreed to the Treaty of Fontainebleau, which ended Napoleon's rule and the Napoleonic Wars, of which the Peninsular War was but one.

The Spanish Constitution of 1812

Battles and bloodshed were not the only things to occur during the Peninsular War. The people of Spain wanted to place their country under an organized government. Delegates came from all over Spain and the Spanish American colonies to voice their opinions.

The Spanish Constitution established a central sovereignty under a constitutional monarchy, the separation of powers, free enterprise, a parliament, and even freedom of the press. The fueros that had been created toward the end of the Muslim occupation were abolished.

The Treaty of Valençay

This treaty was signed on December 11th, 1813. As a result of the agreement, King Ferdinand VII, who had been imprisoned since 1808, was restored as the king of Spain.

As for Napoleon, he managed to resurface in 1815, but it was short-lived. In the end, Napoleon was defeated at Waterloo in modern-day Belgium and was exiled to the island of Saint Helena in the South Atlantic, where he died.

Joseph Bonaparte did well for himself, though. He took a lot of wealth with him from Spain and eventually settled in a sprawling estate in the United States.

The Napoleonic Wars and the Peninsular War essentially cut off Spain from its colonies in the Americas. In addition, the people of the colonies learned how to fend for themselves and rebelled against their colonial masters. The turmoil in Europe and Spain's civil wars bled the economy. Spain, which had once been the world's largest empire, was now struggling to hold on.

Chapter 10 – Aftermath

After the war against Napoleon, Spain was nearly bankrupt. Poverty was widespread, as the battles fought on their soil had destroyed farms, cities, and houses. People, who were desperate by their need to survive, turned to thievery and wandered about, taking what they could. Although there were natural resources, the country lacked the equipment and transportation systems to get it to market.

King Ferdinand VII rejected the 1812 Spanish Constitution because he was desirous of an absolutist regime. The people vehemently opposed him. After fighting long, hard battles, the people had grown more independent and felt that he alone didn't have the skill to organize a country in near ruins.

In 1833, Ferdinand died. Ferdinand's wife, Queen Maria Christiana, became the queen regent, as their daughter, Isabella II, was not yet three years old. However, Ferdinand's brother, Carlos, Count of Molina, disputed her title, wanting the throne for himself. This kicked off the Carlist Wars, which were fought by Carlos and his descendants. The First

Carlist War ended with a Liberal victory. The Liberals were in favor of a progressive government and backed Isabella, while the Carlists wanted a more authoritative regime. The Liberals restored the parliamentary government and reestablished the constitution. When Isabella reached the tender age of thirteen, she became queen in her own right.

In 1846, the powerful Moderate Party, which supported royal power, capitalism, domestic peace, and a strong central government, had sixteen-year-old Isabella II betrothed to Francisco de Asís, her double first cousin. It appears there was no love between the two of them, as Isabella publicly showed her love for General Francisco Serrano in 1847. The Spanish were scandalized. When confronted, she complained about her husband, saying, "What shall I tell you about a man whom I saw wearing more lace than I was wearing on our wedding night?" Serrano wasn't prosecuted, but he was quietly transferred by the government.

In 1851, Isabella gave birth to a daughter, María Isabel. However, things were not rosy in Spain. The following year, a would-be assassin, Martín Merino y Gómez, attempted to stab Isabella. Her dress and corset saved her life, and Martín was executed. This didn't end the people's disgust with the regime.

Spain was subject to other political conflicts. In 1854, Baldomero Espartero, who had a cult following nurtured by the lower classes, became the prime minister again (he had served two terms prior to this), and the government attempted to write a new constitution in 1856. However, the government was unable to complete it because Spain was in utter chaos due to the political wrangling among the Liberals, Moderates, and Republicans. The one cause they all agreed upon was the desire to oust Isabella from power. Isabella II fled to France in 1868, abdicating the throne to her son, Alfonso XII. Many thought he would be controlled by his mother's politics, so, instead, Amadeo, a prince of the House of Savoy, was chosen by the Cortes and became king in 1870. He resigned three years later, saying that the country was "ungovernable." The First Spanish Republic was established the same day, and the country was led by radicals, Democrats, and Republicans.

Spanish-American War (1898)

The people of Cuba wanted independence from Spain, and they started rebelling in 1895 after their first attempts in 1868 didn't pan out. Many in the United States wanted to assist the Cubans for a variety of reasons. Some saw Spain as incapable of governing other territories or believed they were unnecessarily cruel to its people. Others saw opportunities to strengthen economic interests with Cuba. As time passed, more officials in government began calling for war, but President McKinley was uninterested in this. However, he agreed to send support to Cuba to protect American interests.

In 1898, the US sent the USS *Maine* to Havana Harbor. While it was anchored in Havana, there was an enormous explosion onboard. Journalists and War Hawks in the US Congress jumped at the chance to blame Spain, claiming they placed some kind of mine near the ship. To this day, it is not known what caused the explosion, but it is thought to have been due to a coal bunker fire, which was exacerbated by the ship's poor design.

The Explosion of the USS Maine
https://commons.wikimedia.org/wiki/File:Maine_explosion.jpg

The publicity Cuba received in American newspapers revealed the deplorable conditions the Cuban workers were forced to deal with. General Valeriano Weyler y Nicolau, nicknamed "the Butcher," was particularly harsh. President William McKinley was still reluctant to go to war against Spain, and he suggested that America mediate an end to the war. The main issue Cuba wanted to resolve was for Spain to deliver the island nation its independence. However, Spain refused to do so.

The US used its four battleships, the USS *Indiana*, the USS *Massachusetts*, the USS *Iowa*, and the USS *Oregon*. Commodore George Dewey and Major General Wesley Merritt moved their men and ships into Havana Harbor and pummeled the anchored Spanish vessels with gunfire. The war raged on from the end of April 1898 to August 13th, 1898. This loss reduced Spain's power and prestige in the world. Spain relinquished power over Cuba and ceded Puerto Rico, Guam, and the Philippines to the United States. The US also paid $20 million for the damage to the infrastructure owned by Spain.

The Collapse of the Bipartisan Era

After the failed attempt to set up the First Spanish Republic, the monarchy was restored under Alfonso XII in 1874.

By 1913, the country's political parties had splintered into smaller factions, each of which followed a different leader who promoted facets of either conservatism or liberalism. World War I broke out in 1914, but Spain remained neutral. The warring countries demanded products, which was somewhat helpful for the Spanish economy, but the lack of imports that accompanied the war caused a shortage of necessary products.

Political difficulties were heightened when three political parties tried to overthrow the Spanish government. To put an end to the constant fluctuations between a liberal and a parliamentary style monarchy, Miguel

Primo de Rivera took dictatorial power after winning the acquiescence of the king at the time, Alfonso XIII, in 1923. However, by 1930, de Rivera had lost the support of the military, as well as that of the king. He had catered to the elites and heightened social tensions, so he was forced to resign.

In the municipal elections of 1931, there was little support for pro-monarchy parties in the cities. As a result, King Alfonso XIII fled the country, which set the stage for the Second Spanish Republic.

The Second Spanish Republic

In 1931, the Second Spanish Republic was established. Political factionalism was extreme, and people on either side of the fence suspected their opposition was guilty of concocting conspiracies. Even religious attitudes became politicized, as the Church was seen as protecting Spanish values by the conservatives, while leftists viewed the Church as an obstacle to modernity.

In 1933, the Spanish Confederation of the Autonomous Right (CEDA) rose up in strength, and it was powerful enough to quell an armed rebellion in northern Spain. At that time, a far-right movement, the Movimiento Español Sindicalista, arose, which supported fascism.

In 1934, a revolutionary movement took place, which was triggered by the emergence of CEDA. This created antagonism between the right and leftist elements in Spain, which eventually led to a civil war.

Spanish Civil War

In 1936, the political polarization came to a head when Republicans, who were left-leaning and favored leftist factions such as communism, opposed those who favored nationalism. The Nationalists were backed by both monarchical and fascist groups. The Soviet Union helped the Republican side, while Fascist Italy and later Nazi Germany supported the Nationalists.

Before the civil war broke out, a strong-willed man by the name of Francisco Franco had risen in power. He was a Nationalist, but more importantly, having spent his life as a professional soldier, he was an experienced military man. He had witnessed the political chaos that overran the country for nearly a decade, but he preferred strictly observed law and order. To many, he looked stable in the midst of the confusing conglomeration of political ideologies, such as republican democracy, revolution, nationalism, dictatorship, communism, socialism, and monarchy. Others, however, saw him as too controlling.

The Republicans had taken control of the government in 1936 with a very narrow victory. Shortly after, the government moved influential Nationalist figures to distant posts. Franco was sent to the Canary Islands. Emilio Mola y Vidal, the man who was behind the Spanish coup of 1936, was sent to Pamplona. He contacted Franco to see if he was interested in helping take control of Spain. At first, Franco refused, but he later changed his mind. Mola saw to it that Franco was transferred to Spanish Morocco, where he would have access to North African troops. Franco persuaded rightist military officers in Spanish Morocco to rebel so he could gain their loyalty as well.

Their plans were found out, so they had to push forward quickly. The rebels didn't take any major cities except for Seville, where Franco landed his troops.

The Extremadura Campaign

In early August, the Nationalists left Seville and headed toward Badajoz. By August 14th, the Nationalists had gained Mérida and Badajoz. Their next target was Madrid, and it seemed as if nothing could stop them.

The Battle of Irún

Between August 19th and September 5th, 1936, the Nationalists under Lieutenant Colonel Alfonso Beorlegui Canet captured the important city of Irún, cutting off the northern provinces from their source of armaments and support from France.

Initial Siege of Madrid

In November 1936, the Nationalists sieged Madrid. The Republicans were able to hold off the Nationalists temporarily, but the Nationalists kept a partial hold on the University City area. After failing to capture the city, Franco ordered a heavy aerial bombardment, in which the Nazi German Condor Legion assisted. By December, both sides were exhausted. A frontline stabilized in the city, and the bombing became more sporadic. This siege continued throughout the war, only ending in March 1939.

Battle of Guadalajara

Between March 8th and March 23rd, 1937, the Republicans successfully launched a counter-offensive against the Nationalists and their Italian allies, who attempted to encircle Madrid. This was a decisive victory for the Republicans, and it greatly improved morale. It was a great blow to the Italians, though, and to help mitigate the disaster, Franco announced he would disperse the Italian troops, something that he never actually followed through with.

Italian tanks during the Battle of Guadalajara
Bundesarchiv, Bild 183-P0214-516 / CC-BY-SA 3.0, CC BY-SA 3.0 DE

Segovia and Bilbao

In May 1937, the Nationalists were trying to advance toward Bilbao in the north. The Republicans staged a diversionary tactic to stop their progress. They brought in heavy aerial bombardment, but by June 1st, Commander Fernando Barrón of the Nationalists moved in with heavy air support. The Nationalists' air strength proved to be superior to that of the Republicans, who had to retreat on June 6th.

Between June 12th and June 19th, 1937, the Republicans constructed the "iron ring" around Bilbao for defense, but it was poorly made, and the Nationalists easily penetrated it.

The Asturias Offensive

From September 1st to October 21st, 1937, the Republicans tried to delay the Nationalist advance in the north until winter. However, the Nationalists brought in the Condor Legion from Nazi Germany to help with their aerial bombing campaign. By mid-October, the Nationalists broke the Republican front. The Republicans tried to evacuate, but the Nationalists blocked the Asturian harbors and sunk the Republican destroyer, the *Ciscar*. On October 21st, twenty-two Republican battalions surrendered, and the Republicans lost control of the northern regions.

The Aragon Offensive

This campaign took place from March 7th to April 19th, 1938. The Nationalists pounded the Republicans with artillery and aerial bombardments. However, the Republicans were running out of equipment, as aid from the Soviets was drying up. Republican forces were driven back, and the retreat of many fighters left the Republicans in disarray. Toward the end of March, the Nationalists captured the town of Fraga and entered Catalonia.

The Republicans were able to obtain more equipment, but it was too late. By April 19th, the Nationalists held forty miles of the Mediterranean coastline. The Nationalists believed that the war was almost won, but the Republicans would hold on for another year.

Battle of the Ebro

The struggle to control the lower course of the Ebro River lasted from July 25th to November 16th, 1938. At the end of July, the Republicans conducted a large operation to cross the river, doing so mostly at night. They surprised the Nationalist forces on the other side and took 4,000 prisoners on the first day.

Franco then sent in heavy reinforcements. He opened two dams, and the pontoon bridges the Republicans had built were destroyed, but the Republicans managed to repair them in two days. They attempted to take the town of Gandesa but failed when Franco sent in aircraft and heavy artillery.

The heat of August, combined with shortages of food and supplies, weakened the Republicans, but they fought bravely. However, they were unprepared for the superior aircraft of the Nazi Condor Legion and the Italian Aviazione Legionaria, which overwhelmed them.

The Nationalists sent in ground forces after the aerial assault. By November 16th, the Nationalists had regained the territory occupied by the Republicans, scoring another major victory.

The Fall of Madrid

By the spring of 1939, the Republican cause was doomed, and the siege of Madrid had run its course. Even so, the socialist prime minister, Juan Negrín, and other government ministers wanted to fight to the end. However, Republican Colonel Segismundo Casado wanted to negotiate a surrender. He arrested communist officers in Madrid and deposed Negrín, who fled Spain. Madrid was rocked by infighting, with communists and non-communists fighting each other. In the end, the communists were defeated, and their leader, Luis Barceló, was tried by a military tribunal and executed on March 15th.

Casado wanted to negotiate with Francisco Franco, but Franco demanded unconditional surrender. On March 26th, Franco marched into Madrid. The Republican defenses collapsed, and they surrendered two days later. Hundreds of thousands of Republicans were arrested and sent to concentration camps.

Franco was recognized as the head of state by France, Argentina, and Britain in February of 1939. Germany also recognized him but treated him with caution.

The Lost Children

During the Spanish Civil War, the Nationalists abducted children from Republican parents. Any Republican who had been jailed or killed had their children taken from them. Many were adopted by Nationalist couples after being indoctrinated in Francoist principles.

In 1940, women who were imprisoned were sometimes allowed to have their children with them. However, the conditions in the prisons were deplorable. Children of unwed parents were removed and made wards of the state until they reached the age of twenty-five. Their whereabouts after that were often unknown, and human rights groups rose up to resolve the issue but only met with limited success.

It is not known for sure how many children were abducted. Many children were orphaned as a result of the war, and it can be hard to distinguish between that number and those who were taken. The estimate of missing children goes as high as 300,000.

World War II

Soon after the Spanish Civil War ended, another conflict broke out: World War II. Although Franco met with Hitler, he decided upon a policy of neutrality. This was not strictly kept, though. Franco said he would help the Axis, as they helped him during the Spanish Civil War, but

Franco also stationed troops in the Pyrenees to prevent an Axis occupation.

Franco was reluctant to become fully engaged in the war for a number of reasons. Perhaps most importantly, the country had just finished its civil war. Franco needed to focus on stabilizing the economy, which was dependent on the US, before jumping headfirst into a new war. On the other hand, Franco agreed with the political ideologies of Germany and Italy. In 1941, he even allowed volunteers to help the Germans, but only if they fought against the Soviet Union and not the other Allies.

Once the war began to favor the Allies, Franco adhered to a stricter neutrality policy. However, the damage had already been done. When the war was over, Spain was not allowed to join the United Nations, and many countries remained distrustful until about a decade after the war ended.

Francoist Spain

Franco ruled from 1936 until 1975. In the first few decades of his rule, he arrested anyone who opposed him or was known to have opposed him during the war. Prisons became places of death or illness. In 1943, the estimate of people who were killed was approximately 200,000.

The Cortes of the past had no real power; it was just an advisory body. In 1942, the Cortes Españolas was promulgated for legislative purposes. Members of this Cortes could be dismissed by Franco at will, as he was the chief of state and the prime minister, the latter a role he held from 1938 to 1973.

In the 1950s, Franco's rule started to change. It became less violent, although political repression and aggression against his opponents still occurred. In 1954, Franco permitted the Organisation Armée Secrète ("Secret Armed Organization" or OAS) to organize efforts in the French Algerian War since Spain had ties to Spanish Morocco, as it was its protectorate. As a result of that war, Morocco gained its independence, but Spain didn't surrender its control of Spanish Morocco.

When Spain had been occupying southern Morocco, it expanded its holdings in the southwest. This was an area some nomadic Moroccan tribes used. Spain called it "Spanish Sahara." When Morocco gained its independence in 1956, Spain continued to hold Spanish Sahara. Morocco objected to that, claiming that Spanish Sahara (Spanish Morocco) should likewise be surrendered. In the 1960s, Morocco had the United Nations agree that Spain should give up its colonization of the Spanish Sahara; although the UN did so, Spain continued to hold onto the territory.

In 1969, Franco closed the border of Gibraltar. During the War of the Spanish Succession, Great Britain had control of that important region, and Franco was desirous of a contiguous national border for Spain. The people were furious. Thousands were cut off from their families, and it remained isolated from the rest of Spain. In 1982, the border was partially reopened to pedestrians, and it was fully reopened in 1985. The status of Gibraltar is still a hot button issue today.

In 1970, the issue regarding the surrender of the Spanish Sahara (Spanish Morocco) came up again, and Morocco rose up in what is known as the Zemla Intifada ("Zemla Uprising"). Spain suppressed the demonstration, ultimately killing between two to eleven civilians.

In Spain, there had been Catholic trade unions, communist and anarchist groups, liberal organizations, Catalan and Basque separatist movements, and workers' unions—all of these were banned. Members of one group, the Basque Nationalist Party, formed ETA in 1959. ETA was a group that began as a way to fight back against Franco but later turned into a terrorist organization that promoted the Basque culture.

In 1973, Franco resigned as prime minister, as he was getting older, and appointed Luis Carrero Blanco, a Spanish naval officer, to replace him. He was assassinated shortly afterward by ETA, who said, "Carrero

Blanco symbolized better than anyone else 'pure Francoism.'"

When Franco became ill in 1974, he had his heir presumptive, Juan Carlos, take over as acting head of state. Franco returned to office later that year, but he suffered a setback a year later. In late October 1975, Franco went into a coma and was put on life support. On November 20th, his family agreed to take him off life support, and he passed away a few moments later. Two days later, Juan Carlos became the king of Spain.

<u>The Green March</u>

As Franco was becoming more ill, the issue of the Spanish Sahara erupted again. In November of 1975, King Hassan II led an unarmed march of Moroccans to reclaim the area. Spanish troops were sent in, but there was no bloodshed. According to the Madrid Accords that Juan Carlos drew up, Spain agreed to cede the Spanish-held land in exchange for a 35 percent concession to some mines there and offshore fishing rights.

Chapter 11 –Rocky Road to Freedom

King Juan Carlos believed in a constitutional monarchy and wanted to reestablish it. He kept Carlos Arias Navarro as the prime minister, but he became discontented with him, as Arias Navarro operated on the laws of Francoist Spain. There was a power struggle between the two, and eventually, Arias Navarro resigned in 1976. Adolfo Suárez-González replaced him as the new prime minister.

Suárez-González supported the king's interest in making reforms, so he had the Political Reform Act passed in 1977. This law divided the Cortes into two divisions: the Congress, with 350 members, and the Senate, which had 201 members.

A Time of Strikes and Massacres

During Franco's era, various political factions had been suppressed, but all awoke and rose up again to gain power after his death. At the beginning of 1977, a right-wing extremist group who wasn't in favor of reform sent an assassination squad after Joaquín Navarro, who was the general secretary of the transport union in Atocha, because of a strike he started. They entered his office, and although they couldn't find Navarro, they proceeded to kill everyone they found there. Five people died, and the psychological impact was great. This horrendous incident was called the Atocha massacre.

The killers were apprehended in March, as was the conspirator who ordered the killings. They were all imprisoned. Writing about the massacre, a journalist, Juancho Dumall, penned these words, "It was a terroristic act that marked the future of the country in a way that the murderers would not have suspected and, instead, was the one desired by the victims."

Independent labor unions started to form, even though labor unions were still forbidden under the monarchy. Demands for improved working conditions caused a great deal of tumult. Some were overanxious for change, while others were determined to keep the status quo. A young man, Arturo Ruiz, was murdered by an anti-communist on January 23rd, 1977, while protesting for the freedom of political prisoners. Police responded with gas canisters, but they accidentally killed a student in the process.

Gunmen who opposed Francoist policies kidnapped Emilio Villaescusa Quilis, the president of the Supreme Council of Military Justice. They claimed to be leftists, but others indicate that they may have been a part of GRAPO (the "First of October Antifascist Resistance Groups"). Strikes were proclaimed throughout most of the country, including the Asturian areas, the Basque Country, Catalonia, and Madrid. Since so many university students and teachers engaged in the protests, they had to stop classes.

Once the PCE, the non-Soviet aligned Communist Party of Spain, was legalized in April 1977, it proved instrumental in promoting peaceful protests rather than armed conflicts.

Finally, Elections!

The newly formed Spanish government had a number of political parties:

The *Pacte Democràtic per Catalunya* (the "Democratic Pact for Catalonia")

The Communist Party of Spain

The Union of the Democratic Centre, a right-wing party

The Spanish Socialist Workers' Party

The Basque Nationalist Party

The People's Alliance, a right-wing, pro-Francoist party

The Christian Democratic Party

The Basque and Catalan separatists

Advertisements of various political parties

The Spanish Constitution of 1978

This constitution established Spain as a democratic state subject to a set of laws, and it holds to the main principles of liberty, justice, political pluralism, and equality. According to the Spanish Constitution, sovereignty rests with the people. The government is ruled by an executive, the role of the monarch is regulated, and people's fundamental rights and duties are delineated. It set up a justice department and a legislature, which is called the Cortes Generales. Principles that guide the economy and finances are also defined.

Spain is a heavily decentralized country. Some communities are considered autonomous, like the Basque Country, Catalonia, and the province of Galicia. Other significant autonomous communities include Aragon, Navarre, Castile, and León. There are seventeen autonomous communities in all.

Modern Spanish Leaders

Felipe González

In 1982, Felipe González became the prime minister. He ran as a member of the Spanish Socialist Workers' Party. Under his leadership, several liberal measures were passed, such as the legalization of abortion, an increase in personal freedom, and a comprehensive educational program.

The Basque separatist group under Herri Batasuna was banned, as it supported ETA, which was a terrorist group. The Batasuna association used to be elected in Spain. It often blocked the passage of laws, as, due to their abstentions, less than a majority could vote on critical issues. The elimination of the Batasunas eased up legislative performance.

During González's term, there was a huge strike that crippled the economy, as seven million people went on strike for one day on December 14th, 1988. People objected to the very liberal nature of the new reforms. As a result, new elections were held in 1989. González was reelected, and his parliamentary support remained the same.

González served as the prime minister until 1996.

José María Aznar

Aznar was elected prime minister in 1996. He ran as a member of the People's Party, which was a Christian democratic party. During his term, Aznar's government focused its efforts on the economy, and it introduced a number of reforms, not all of which were popular. There was an increase in the price of gasoline, butane, and tobacco. Those increases, in turn, raised prices in sectors that were reliant upon those industries. The purpose of this measure was to be able to start using the euro as currency in Spain. The value of it fluctuated, dropping to $.83 (compared to the US dollar's worth of $1.60) in 2008. Once the figures from the European sovereign-debt crisis was factored in, there was a need for the European Stability Facility, which was created in 2010 to help combat the crisis, to strengthen the Spanish economy.

Aznar did not oversee the debt crisis, as he left office in 2004. But memorable events still occurred. During his term, there was a large general strike due to labor policies the workers considered unfair, and the introduction of the National Hydrologic Plan took place, which provided water more equally to all the provinces. There was a reform of universities, the Spanish support of the US war on Iraq (including the sending of Spanish forces to Iraq), and the poor management of an accident having to do with an oil carrier named the *Prestige*.

In 2002, the *Prestige* spilled 17.8 million US gallons of fuel into the waters off the coast of Galicia in northwestern Spain. The Spanish port refused to permit the ship to dock, as did the neighboring countries of France and Portugal. The spill polluted thousands of miles of coastlines, killing fish. In the end, the old ship broke apart, releasing all of its oil in the process. Of course, this caused a severe problem for fishermen and the environment in general, and Spain had to undergo many expenses to clean it up.

In 2004, a large terrorist attack occurred three days before the elections. It happened at a train station, and it killed 193 people. One of the candidates, José Luis Rodríguez Zapatero, blamed ETA, a Basque separatist group, announcing this to several newspapers, even after an Arab audiotape was later found in the area. Various citizens blamed the People's Party, and others blamed different groups. This was followed by a number of illegal political demonstrations.

On March 14th, 2004, the election was held, and José Luis Rodríguez Zapatero was elected.

José Luis Rodríguez Zapatero

Zapatero had the Spanish withdraw its troops from Iraq, causing a strain on its relations with the US. However, he did see an improvement of relations with Germany and France, who were in opposition to that war. Same-sex marriage was approved during his term. The Catholic Church and some conservatives vehemently opposed it.

Before coming into office, Zapatero made many promises, including the availability of more housing; bi-lingual education (Spanish and English), along with any regional language like *Euskara*, the language of the Basques; computers for students; a two-year limit for legal processes; and the creation of a state-owned TV station that is directly answerable to the Parliament.

In terms of foreign relations, Zapatero traveled to Venezuela and Cuba to improve relations. The US objected, particularly when Zapatero agreed to sell aircraft and ships to Venezuela for military purposes.

At an Iberian-American summit in 2007, Zapatero was often interrupted by Hugo Chavez of Venezuela, a situation that riled the temper of Spain's king, Juan Carlos I, who asked, "¿Por que no te callas?" ("Why don't you shut up?"), and left the meeting. Zapatero later made an impassioned speech about respecting the leaders of other countries.

Spain slammed into a financial crisis in 2008. Firstly, it didn't meet the minimum financial limit of a 3 percent deficit limit, so it wasn't able to bail itself out. In fact, Zapatero had to apply for a 100-billion-euro rescue package. The greatest cause, according to financial analysts, was a housing bubble in combination with a very high GDP (gross domestic product) growth rate, which experts felt was unsustainable. It is believed the housing bubble could have been caused by the loose regulations on banks, which permitted them to hide gains and losses. Initially, tax revenues were high, but that was short-lived because many companies subsequently went bankrupt, and the unemployment rate rose.

Zapatero was succeeded by Mariano Rajoy from the People's Party in 2011.

Mariano Rajoy

Mariano Rajoy won a landslide election. He came to office during the financial crisis that had started in 2008. As a result, austerity measures were put into place. Spending cuts were severe, and changes to the labor law triggered at least two strikes a year.

The revelation of a scandal involving the financing of political parties was brought to light. This marred Rajoy's term, along with the issue of Catalan independence.

Catalonia became an autonomous community after the passage of the Spanish Constitution in 1978. In 2017, Catalonia applied for total independence from Spain, proposing that in the form of a referendum. Rajoy denounced it and then suspended the proposal of the referendum until it could be ruled by the Constitutional Court. This move was extremely unpopular. To make matters worse, Rajoy threatened to take over the finances of Catalonia. He sent out police to raid the Catalan headquarters in Barcelona, and fourteen Catalan officials were arrested. The referendum vote was held anyway, but the voter turnout was too low, making the vote invalid. Physical confrontations between police and protestors occurred, resulting in injuries on both sides. The president of Catalonia, Carles Puigdemont, suspended the issue of independence in exchange for having talks with Spain.

The Catalan Parliament unilaterally decided to declare independence with the support of Puigdemont, who approved the passage of a referendum to that effect. The Spanish government invoked the Constitution to remove regional authorities and enact direct rule. Puigdemont and his Cabinet fled to Belgium, and nothing else came from the Catalan independence movement.

Pedro Sánchez, leader of the Spanish Socialist Workers' Party, proposed a motion of no confidence because of the kickback schemes exposed in a case brought against Rajoy. He lost his seat on a vote of no confidence from his party, which resulted in Sánchez becoming the next prime minister.

Pedro Sánchez

Pedro Sánchez is a strong supporter of the European Union and is active in European affairs.

In 2018, he provided sanctuary for immigrants from an aid group called SOS Mediterranee Sea and Doctors Without Borders. They had been sent back from ports in Italy and Malta because of Europe's growing anti-migrant policies. Sánchez's foreign minister at the time, Josep Borrell, said that Spain was looking for "new blood."

Sánchez wants to reopen the issue related to Catalan independence. However, he did warn the people there that if violence breaks out, he will deploy the police.

In 2019, Sánchez's budget was rejected, and he called for a general election, saying that "Spain needs to keep advancing, progressing with tolerance, respect, moderation and common sense." His party won the election.

Sánchez made a major change to the government when he incorporated members of different parties as deputy prime ministers. Today, the Cabinet includes members of the Spanish Socialist Workers' Party (Sánchez's party) and the Unidas Podemos, a left-wing party, as well as representatives from other parties.

In 2020, the Spanish government announced the merger of two banks, Bankia and CaixaBank, but warned that competition must be respected.

The current king of Spain is Felipe VI, and Spain has the thirteenth largest economy in terms of its GDP. Spain has had a rough journey through history, but it has certainly come a long way.

Conclusion

Because of its ideal location on the Atlantic Ocean, Spain has been vulnerable ever since the Iberian tribes inhabited its lands. From all their overlords and foreign governors, the Spanish learned what was valuable. For instance, they learned architectural and military styles from the Romans. Yet their hardy and courageous tribes resisted domination to their dying breath, like the Celtiberians, who chose suicide rather than slavery, or the Numantines, who were willing to die rather than surrender. They minted coins for the Romans and the Visigoths, but they always had the names of their towns or their tribes engraved upon them.

Spain has had its fair share of monarchs and dictators. Today, Spain's constitutional monarchy promotes equality, freedom, and pluralism. It is noted for its autonomous communities, including the historical regions of the Basque County, Galicia in the northwest, and Catalonia.

Spain has one of the largest economies in the world, and it has come a long way since its beginnings as a primarily farming country. Today, tourism is one of its greatest attractions, as Spain has carefully preserved its historical sites and is noted for its beautiful beaches and winter resorts.

Part 2: The Basques

A Captivating Guide to the History of the Basque Country, Starting from Prehistory through Roman Rule and the Middle Ages to the Present

Introduction

The Basques live in a portion of the Pyrenees in the far southwestern corner of France and across the ridge in the north-central portion of Spain, centered on the towns of Pamplona and Donostia. While some live outside this area today, many still call this region home. These hardy people have dwelt in the foothills of the jagged Pyrenees Mountains since prehistoric times, and they're still there to this day.

The Basques manifest a genetic makeup that is prehistorically distinct from that of their neighbors in Spain or France. This has puzzled scientists and researchers for years. A genetic study conducted by Uppsala University in Sweden in 2015 discovered that the Basques established themselves as an ethnic group during Neolithic times, anywhere from 12,000 to 4,500 years ago.

The Basques were isolated from other human migrations into Europe for millennia. Anthropologists have said that they are descendants of the Neolithic farmers who intermingled with a hunter-gatherer culture. About 850,000 pure Basques live in Spain, while 130,000 dwell in France.

Their language is unique; it is a "language isolate," meaning it has no genealogical relationship with other languages. It is not one of the "Romance" languages, that is, derived from Latin. It is not derived from the Indo-European family of languages either, which is characteristic of Germany, Europe, or the Slavic countries.

The principal propelling agent for the success of the Basques throughout the ages is the people's need for survival. For generations, the Basques lived in the foothills and mountains of the Pyrenees. They learned how to harness that challenging terrain and make it their own.

In Spain, the Basques mainly live in the Southern Basque Country, which is composed of three provinces. Álava (or Araba-Álava), Biscay (or Vizcaya), and Gipuzkoa are autonomous Spanish Basque communities, which means they have their own administration and political organizations, as well as their own leaders, legislatures, courts, and assemblies. Navarre is also an autonomous community, but it has separated itself from the other three provinces. They continue to have a relationship with the country of Spain in terms of taxation and tariffs.

In France, many Basques live in the Northern Basque Country, also called the French Basque Country. It lays west of the Pyrénées-Atlantique. The Northern Basque Country incorporates the three historical Basque provinces of Labourd, Soule, and Lower Navarre. In 2017, a single commonwealth was created in France for the French Basque Country, and it is known as the Agglomerate Community of Basque Country. The French Basque Country is also called *Iparralde.* In Basque, it means the "northern region."

There is also a diaspora of Basque, who mostly live in France, Spain, the United States South America, and a curious collection of French islands called Saint Pierre and Miquelon.

A great effort has been made here to present the clearest explanation possible to elucidate the history of these fascinating people. However, through the ravages of history and its turnover of conquerors, the borders of the Basque lands have shifted, and the names of places have changed with unnerving frequency.

Chapter 1 – The Mystery of the Mountain People

The Basque Country

The greater Basque Country, also known as *Euskal Herria* (the oldest documented name for the home of the Basques), is located in the northeastern corner of Spain and southwestern France. The region is about three million square miles, and it is home to around three million inhabitants. It is a mountainous country in the Pyrenees, but the heights of the jagged mountain peaks do not exceed 3,500 feet. In the winter, the mountaintops are covered with snow. The terrain slopes down into the fertile valley of the Ebro River.

The Basques have beaches made of either sand or rocks. The mountains have many caverns, some of which contain paintings of bears rendered by early man. There are forests in this region as well, and the southern region of the Basque Country even has a desert. The weather is cool and damp in the north, as it lies on the coast of the northern Atlantic.

Today, the Basque Country is known as the cultural region of the Basques, and it is split into three areas: the Basque Autonomous Community in Spain, the Chartered Community of Navarre, and *Iparralde*, or the French Basque Country. The northern provinces border the Bay of Biscay. "Bisc" and its variation of "Visc" stands for Vascones (or Viscones), the largest historical tribe of the Basques.

The Basque cultural region consists of provinces that have large numbers of Basques living among people from other cultures, mainly those of French and Spanish backgrounds. Those provinces are Labourd (*Lapurdi*), Lower Navarre (*Nafarroa Beherea*), and Soule (*Zuberoa*). The most common language of the Basque Autonomous Community is *Euskara*. Others outside of the region simply call it the Basque language. The cultural region also has some who speak French or Spanish, in addition to speaking Basque.

Mysterious Origins

Archaeological investigations seem to indicate the earliest hominids arrived in the Basque Country during the Paleolithic era, more specifically between 43,000 and 23,000 years ago, possibly even earlier. The Paleolithic era, also known as the Old Stone Age, refers to the first prehistorical period in which humans developed stone tools. It coincides with what is called the Pleistocene, or the Ice Age, at which time the glaciers started to recede.

It appears that humans migrated from Eastern Europe to Western Europe and eventually to the Basque Country. Their culture was called the Aurignacian. The skeletal remains of *Homo antecessor* and *Homo heidelbergensis*, along with primitive tools, were found in a cave called the El Portalón in Atapuerca, Spain. *Homo heidelbergensis* is the oldest human fossil in the world. Some believe that *Homo neanderthalensis* ("Neanderthals") descended from *Homo heidelbergensis*. However, the existence of *Homo heidelbergensis* as a separate species is highly debatable. Relationships between these archaic, now extinct species are unclear, but they were ancestors of *Homo sapiens*, which are modern humans.

In the Cantabrian region, which lies just west of the current-day Basque Country, rock art was discovered in a cave in Aitzbitarte Hill, dating back to the Paleolithic era. In the Isturitz and Oxocelhaya caverns in the Basque Country, located in the province of Navarre, human bones were also found, specifically cranial vaults used as drinking vessels, bone flutes, and cave paintings of lion cubs and oxen. Navarre in is the Pyrenees, near the French border.

The Santimamiñe Cave in the Basque Country displays cave art of not only bison, wooly mammoths, wooly rhinoceroses, horses, and bears—it also shows pictures of lions. Fossil remains of lions dating back from 191,000 to 11,700 years ago were actually found in Europe from the Pleistocene period. In fact, this cave contains the complete skeleton of a lion. Lions and rhinoceroses have never been seen in the wilds of Western Europe during recorded history, especially in the colder mountain regions. However, it is quite possible that the ancient Basques hunted lions. The Santimamiñe Cave, where those fossils were found, is near the coast of the Bay of Biscay, west of the French border in the Pyrenees.

In the Gatzarria Cave in the French Pyrenees, which lies east of the Basque Country, there are remnants of the carcasses of red deer and bison. There is evidence of the existence of Neanderthals at this site, but the general consensus is that the human population there was less dense.

Differences between the Iberians and the Basques

As indicated in the studies reported in the Proceedings of the National Academy of Sciences of the United States of America, Torsten Gunther and other researchers of Uppsala University in Sweden discovered that ancient Iberian farmers mixed with the "hunter-gatherers" who were already in the Basque Country between 25 million to 12,000 years ago during the Paleolithic era. Iberians were the ancient people who lived in today's countries of Spain and Portugal—the Iberian Peninsula, in other words.

The origin of the Basques is controversial to this day. Language is frequently used as a tool by anthropologists to discover the origin of a society. However, linguists have already seen differences between the Basque language and the Iberian language. In addition, they also have discovered that the Basque language differs from other Indo-European languages. Linguistic analyses conclude that the Basque language may be related to that of the hunter-gatherers who preceded the agriculturally-oriented Basques, who came in during the Neolithic times. Their language is truly unique. Because efforts to find similarities in the Basque language and the ancient Iberian language have failed, the two groups were initially distinct from one another when the Basques settled the land. The Basque language, or *Euskara* as the Basques call it, is a language isolate, which is a unique language that is very unlike the languages spoken in neighboring lands. In order to determine the origin of an ethnic group, scientists use not only genetic factors but also language. Members of the same tribe often speak the same tongue, and that generally continues to be spoken throughout the generations. As they mix and mingle with other tribes over time, though, new words and new pronunciations infiltrate.

However, there is still an unanswered question. Who were the hunter-gatherers who spoke the Basque language and preceded the Iberian farmer migrants into the Basque Country?

DNA studies conducted by the Genographic Project for the National Geographic Society have shown that the genetic structure of the Basque people is different from that of the Iberians. Also, ancient Iberians populated Spain abound 7,000 years ago, placing them in the Mesolithic/Neolithic era (the Middle/Late Stone Age). The Basques, however, appear to have originated in the Paleolithic era, thus predating the Iberians. Those who were called "Iberians" arrived after the Basques. In fact, the DNA studies on the Basques show they are *not* of Indo-European origin, while the Iberians are.

Geneticists have analyzed Basque mitochondrial DNA and discovered that there are similar chromosomal markers and other DNA evidence from people from the Ural Mountains of Russia. They are attempting to discover if there is a relationship between the two, but evidence for that determination is unclear at the moment.

To sum up, the origin of the Basques is an enigma, and only time will tell if more information arises to help dispel the mists surrounding their murky beginnings.

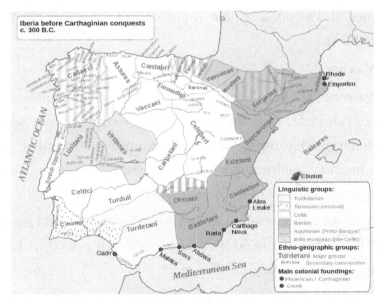

Basque tribes in the Iberian Peninsula
Alcides Pinto, GFDL <http://www.gnu.org/copyleft/fdl.html>, via Wikimedia Commons
https://commons.wikimedia.org/wiki/File:Iberia_300BC-en.svg

The Basque Tribes

The early tribes of the Basques were known as the Vascones, the Autrigones, the Caristii, the Varduli, the Vescetani, the Iacentani, the Tarbelli, the Suburates, the Biguerres, and the Aquitanians. Territories occupied by the Tarbelli, the Suburates, the Biguerres, and the Aquitanians lay within the southwestern portion of current-day France. In his book, *Commentaries on the Gallic Wars* (published between 58 and 49 BCE), Julius Caesar noted that their land "looks between the setting sun and the North Star." Although Caesar noted them in his book, he was far from the first to talk about them. The earliest written history of that area coincided with the arrival of the Roman Empire in 196 BCE, prior to Caesar's reign.

Through history, the term "Vascones" has come to be associated with the Basques, but there is no evidence that the Vascones were the ancestors of today's Basques. Some of the ancient tombstones from the Roman era bear names of Vascones, so that is just one of the terms the Romans applied to them.

The Vascones

The Vascones has been referred to as a tribe, but the etymological root "Vasco" can also refer to all the Basques. The word "Vascones" was often used interchangeably with "Basques" throughout recorded history, although linguistic analyses show a strong similarity between the proto-Basque language and that of the Aquitanians, a French tribe.

The Vascones were referred to by ancient historians like Livy around 76 BCE, Pliny the Elder in 50 BCE, and Strabo between 63 BCE and 14 CE during the reign of Augustus Caesar.

The term "Vascones" also came to be synonymous with the Basques because of cultural and linguistic similarities. Through linguistic analysis, it has been determined the language spoken by the prehistorical Vascones was "proto-Basque," meaning it predated the current Basque language, *Euskara.*

When the Romans came raging in, the Vascones reached an agreement with Julius Caesar by granting Rome access to Iberia, allowing the Romans to go from Gaul (France), over the Pyrenees, and through their territory. As part of their agreement, the Vascones weren't subjected to heavy colonization by the Romans during the Roman Republic. Instead, they were recruited by the ancient Romans as mercenary soldiers.

The Aquitanians

Aquitania was a tribal nation consisting of a number of sub-tribes. The western portion of Aquitania became part of the Basque Country. When the earliest people inhabited this land, they were hunters. Archaeological evidence of Aquitanian art shows figures of extinct animals such as the wooly mammoth and the tarpan. The tarpan was a wild horse that was smaller than today's horse. Besides these extinct species, the Aquitanians hunted bison, deer, and goats. They had oxen and boars, and they were one of the earliest people to domesticate the dog.

Although prehistoric Aquitanians did become farmers, agriculture arrived very late, and it wasn't widespread until later. It may have occurred toward the end of the Neolithic period during the New Stone Age some 12,000 years ago. Some historians, though, contradict that opinion based on genetic evidence. They believe that it coincided with the Early Iron Age instead. Today, agriculture is the secondary occupation of these hardy people. Technology is their primary occupation now.

Julius Caesar describes the Aquitanian tribe in his famed book, *Commentaries on the Gallic Wars.* One of the most-quoted lines in his book is about the Aquitanians: "All Gaul is divided into three parts, one of which the Belgae inhabit, and the Aquitani another." The Belgae were a collection of tribes living in Gaul. Aquitania was in southwestern "Celtica," the early Roman word for France. The Aquitanians were sometimes called "Gallia Belgica," meaning "long-haired Gaul." Caesar divided the Aquitanian land into "Aquitania Prima" in the northeast, "Aquitania Secunda" in the central region, and "Aquitania Tertia" in the southwest.

During their campaign to conquer the Iberian Peninsula, the Romans fought many battles against the Aquitanian tribe. However, they did occupy some areas there and set up settlements. The Basque tribes realized they wouldn't be subject to Roman law, and they were able to keep their culture and customs intact.

The Autrigones

Strabo called the Autrigones the "Allótrigones," a word that means "strange people." He also added that "the rough and savage manners of these people is not alone owing to their wars, but likewise to their isolated position." Strabo was referring to the 4th century BCE when the Autrigones overran Cantabria and Burgos, which were territories just to their west.

The Caristii and Varduli Tribes

The Caristii occupied an area along the coast of the Bay of Biscay off the northern coast of Spain. The Santimamiñe Cave is located there. There is no indication of any resistance to the Roman occupation by these two tribes. In fact, the Varduli served as mercenaries during the Roman period. They even assisted the Romans in the conquest of Britannia.

The Iacentani

The Iacentani people were a sub-tribe of the Aquitanians. In 195 BCE, they were overwhelmed by the Vescetani people (see below), who devastated and sacked their towns and lands. The Iacentani lands were then annexed and made part of the territory of the Vescetani.

The Vescetani

These people could have been the Aquitanian tribe that dwelled on the northern tributary of the Ebro River. The Vescetani may have been part of the Celtic migration into the northern Pyrenees territory around 600 BCE. The Vescetani cooperated with the Roman conquest but later rebelled. Under Commander Gaius Terentius Varro, they were vanquished, and the Romans took over their territory.

They may have been assimilated into the territory of the Vascones by the 2nd century BCE because their names do not appear in the ancient texts of Ptolemy or Strabo.

The Tarbelli

The Tarbelli dwelled in today's province of Labourd in the French Basque Country. Linguists have identified their dialect as being related to that of the Aquitanians. Julius Caesar called them the "Tarbelli of the four banners," meaning they consisted of four subtribes.

The Suburates

Ancient history indicates that this tribe inhabited the current-day province of Soule in the French Basque Country. Like the Tarbelli, they were related to the Aquitanians. Julius Caesar also mentions them as having surrendered some hostages as a token of submission to the conquering Romans.

The Biguerres

The Biguerres were one of the Aquitanian tribes that surrendered to Marcus Licinius Crassus, Caesar's lieutenant. The origin of the term "Biguerres" might have come from the word "ibai gorri," which means "red river." It could have been referring to the Garonne River that runs through Aquitaine, as that river has a distinctive brownish-red tinge.

Neighboring Tribes

The Cantabrians

During the Bronze Age, around the year 2500 BCE, some Celts came to the Basque Country. Some of them settled in the western Iberian Peninsula, but others migrated northeast to the coast. Some intermarried with the indigenous Basques.

According to Roman Senator Cato the Elder, the main river of Cantabria was the Ebro River, which runs through the Pyrenees. He stated, "The Ebro River starts in the land of Cantabri, large and beautiful, with abundant fish."

The Cantabrians spoke a very early form of the Celtic language as opposed to *Euskara*, the language of the Basques. Although the Cantabrians were once considered to be one of the early Basque tribes, it is now known that their origin isn't Basque; it is Celtic. In Roman times, the Cantabrians inhabited an area just west of the Basque regions.

The Astures

The Astures dwelled west of Cantabria, along the coast of the Bay of Biscay. They were matrilineal, which means women were considered to be the heads of the household. They inherited money and even fought in wars alongside men.

Chapter 2 – The Ancient Mystery Unravels

Basques in the Chalcolithic Era

"Chalcolithic" is the term applied to the Copper Age, which was the era just preceding the Bronze Age. The earliest artifacts from the Chalcolithic Age in the Basque Country have been dated to around 2500 BCE.

The people sought to develop tools more malleable than stone. Copper was mined in the Basque region, which can be melted so that it is soft enough to hammer into tools. Once it is mixed with tin, it becomes bronze.

The Basques created "bell beakers," as did other Iberian peoples. Bell beakers were common in the Western Pyrenees, which includes the Basque territory. The bell beaker, which was made from terracotta clay, was shaped like a wide vase. Some of those bell beakers were used to heat up fresh copper. The bell beakers were also used as drinking vessels—although they were rather large ones—from which the Basques drank mead, a fermented honey wine. The bell beakers were also used to hold grain or other foods and drinks. The pottery during this time was undecorated.

The Basques in the Bronze Age

The Bronze Age covered the period of 1700 to 700 BCE. Bronze wasn't as plentiful in the Basque territory, and it was mostly used for practical uses, such as cooking pots, or in fortifications and ornamentation. The Basques had a prolonged Bronze Age in comparison to the surrounding areas. This was due to their isolation.

The pottery made by the Basques during the Bronze Age became more highly decorated. A lot of it was "corded," meaning the creator would make ropes out of plant fibers and twist them up into a cord. The cords would be wrapped around the vessel. After they were removed, a decorative impression was left behind. They are sometimes called "cordons."

Bronze tools and weapons were also made, including axes, spears, and arrowheads.

Basque Burial Customs

To commemorate their dead, the prehistorical Basques built dolmens, which are monuments consisting of two immense vertical stones supporting a horizontal stone. These were mostly made of limestone, which was the most common stone in the Basque Country. Most Basque graves were common graves, but some had chambers. As one might expect, people from the higher classes were buried in the graves with more than one chamber. By the Iron Age, bodies were cremated.

It was important that the burials be made close to the villages that the people once inhabited. Some families even buried their loved ones beneath their homes.

In later years, after the Basques were Christianized, they were buried near the churches they attended. Crosses were carved on their tombstones. Bells sounded for funerals, and the knelling was different for men than for women. The mourners were expected to make donations to the grieving family, especially if the deceased had very young children. At weddings, it was customary for the bride and groom to visit the gravesites of their close relatives. It was a way in which the family was "introduced" to the new couple. The bride would bring candles and flowers to symbolize respect and love for those who had died.

When the family visited the graves of loved ones, they might leave a piece of wood carved in the shape of a person and coated with wax.

The Basques in the Iron Age

The Iron Age, which followed the Bronze Age, arrived in the Basque Country around 600 BCE. Burial customs changed during that timeframe. Instead of collective burials in mounds, bodies were cremated and then buried inside stone circles called cromlechs.

During the Iron Age, the Basques became more agricultural. Cereal crops, like millet, wheat, and quinoa, were grown.

Basque Mythology and Religion

Each village had its own gods and goddesses. One of the more popular goddesses was Mari, the main goddess of the Basque religion. She was the "earth mother." Mari was symbolized by a round disk called the *luburu.* When the great goddess was in her underground dwelling, she was displayed in an animal form, which was either a horse, goat, or vulture. The Basques lived in the mountains, and they saw caves as safe places to dwell.

When she was displayed during the day, Mari was depicted as a long-haired, beautiful woman in a red tunic with a dragon at her feet. Mari held a golden crown in her right hand. Her consort was Sugaar, and Mari occasionally would join Sugaar to create storms. These storms were beneficial to the people because they brought much-needed rain for their crops, although sometimes they were destructive. Sugaar was sometimes represented as a male serpent. Mari and Sugaar had two sons: Atarrabi (or Atxular), who represents good, and Mikelats, who represents evil.

The Basque creation story is very similar to those told by other cultures around the world. In the beginning, there was nothing but darkness. Then Mari gave birth to a daughter, Ilargi, the moon. When Mari's people complained that the moon did not give sufficient light, Mari gave birth to another daughter, who was Eguzki, the sun.

At night, the terrors that haunt the land were sometimes extreme, so Mari gave her people the flower of the sun, which was known as the Eguzkilore. It was a flower that resembled a thistle. She advised her people to display this flower on their doors to protect them from the specters of the night.

The Basques followed a Chthonic cult. It promoted the belief in an underworld. The underworld they ascribed to wasn't necessarily beneath the earth per se; it was more like a place for the undercurrent of deities, which influenced people and events. The Basques cherished many legends, some of which contained beings called *mairuak*, who were the giant builders of their grave monuments, cromlechs, and stone circles. The *jentilak* was a race of powerful giants who built megalithic monuments. The *iratxoak* were imps, the *sorginak* referred to witches and priestesses, and the *basajaunak* were the wild men and women of the woods.

During medieval times, a local Basque legend relates that the Basques were descendants of Tubal, the grandson of Noah. Tubal was one of the sons of Japheth. Japheth and Tubal came from an ancient biblical tribe that departed Mesopotamia and settled in Iberia along the Ebro River.

Over the years, even during the prehistorical era, tales about the gods and goddesses have changed. In the town of Biarritz, in Labourd province, for example, the people taught that Mari did not dwell in the cave; she dwelt on the highest mountains. That legend instructs the people that Mari divided the people into two groups: the people who lived during the day—the *egunekoak*—and the people who lived at night—the *gauekoak*. The people weren't always seen as human; they were disembodied beings or spirits of the dead.

Death in the Basque Mythology

First of all, the Basques focused on the importance of a "good death." According to a prominent Basque anthropologist, Annuntxi Arana, oral stories were passed on from generation to generation, and they highlighted the fact that a "good death" implied that the person lived a good life. Prayers on behalf of the dying person were essential to keeping the evil spirits at bay. A "bad death," meaning a violent death, was the work of magical intervention. Another sign of a bad or troubled death was the weather close to the time of one's passing.

People often used amulets to protect themselves from the evil spirits that were attracted to those who were dying.

Mythical entities called *lamiak* were good spirits who dwelled near waterways. They were the opposite of the mythological sirens from Greek mythology, who allowed men's ships to crash on the rocky shore. Instead, the *lamiak* would aid people when they were in need as long as the supplicants left gifts. *Lamiak* were believed to help in the birth of a child. They were also summoned when someone was about to die so they could help aid them. They were, in essence, "good witches."

Kind women existed outside of myths as well. At times, women provided herbal remedies to ease the pain of suffering. They rendered their services not only for those who were dying but also for those who simply needed some kind of treatment.

The early Basques believed specters and symbols of death would visit people to alert them to an impending death, whether it was their own death or that of someone close to them. Some typical death omens were a cock crowing during the night or the incessant barking of dogs.

In some interpretations, the Basque goddess Mari dwelled in the world of the dead—a cave, if you will. She symbolized the passage of a person moving from the land of the living into the underworld. It should be noted the Basque underworld was not seen as a negative place like Hell. Instead, it was the cave of the spirits. The dead could be resurrected into the land of the living as a breath or a gentle wind, and they could live comfortably among the living. However, if a person left a serious matter unresolved, that might conjure up their spirit into the waking world. These visitations were sometimes accompanied by strange noises at night, and the person who was being "warned" was expected to find some way of making restitution for his or her offense.

The Afterlife

According to the Basques, when a person died, they were transformed into another mode of existence. If their life was a good one, they would go down the path into the underworld and into Mari's cave. Then they would be led to a land of peace, abundance, and overwhelming happiness. If they had committed offenses during their life, and as long as those offenses were not too numerous or severe, they were made to wander for a while in the dark, seeking Mari's cave. When they found it, they were welcomed in. However, if a person was truly evil, he or she would be forced to wander about in the darkness, harassed by evil spirits forever.

The cave utilized in the Basque mythology relates to their early prehistory, during which time they needed to take shelter from the glaciers or weather through the storms. For the prehistoric Basques, caves were safe places.

Chapter 3 – The Basques under the Roman Empire

The Basques during the Punic Wars and the Roman Conquest

In the 3rd century BCE, Carthage, a port city in North Africa, was interested in trade and wanted to expand so it could include colonies surrounding the Mediterranean. In 246 BCE, Carthage became involved in a massive conflict with Rome, which was also expanding. These clashes were known as the "Punic" Wars, after the Roman term for Carthage. There were three Punic Wars altogether.

Although the Vascones once worked for the Romans as mercenaries, during the Punic Wars, they fought on the side of the Carthaginians. Therefore, the Basque tribes weren't always mercenaries for Rome. It all depended upon the circumstances under which they were hired and the year of the engagements.

The Carthaginians annexed and colonized cities around the Mediterranean Sea and established the Carthaginian Empire. Between the years 237 and 218 BCE, the Carthaginians boldly infiltrated the Iberian Peninsula and traveled northward. Upon reaching the areas in the far north, they encountered the Basques. The Carthaginians weren't interested in settling the Basque Country, which they called "Vasconia," but they depended upon the Basques to become mercenaries to help them conquer new lands. Many able-bodied Vascones readily accepted that role and were paid in gold and silver. In 216 BCE, the Vascones marched with Hannibal across the Alps and into Italy. Hannibal, though, was unable to march on Rome itself because he lacked siege engines.

The city of Carthage itself was destroyed in 146 BCE, and once the Vascones and other Basque tribes saw that destruction, they were reluctant to go up against the Romans ever again.

The Sertorian War

The Romans brought their civil war with them when they occupied Spain. Between the years 88 and 80 BCE, two Roman consuls, Gaius Marius and Lucius Cornelius Sulla, opposed each other, as both wanted full control of the Roman territories.

Quintus Sertorius was the governor of Hispania. He was considered a moderate governor, and he treated the conquered people fairly. Because of political conflicts in Italy, Serortius became a rebellious Roman.

Sertorius supported the Marian faction, but when Sulla won the civil war and became a tyrant in Rome, Sulla sent a force to Hispania to defeat Sertorius and his supporters. Sertorius then fled to Tingis in North Africa (near Morocco). To his surprise, Sertorius was met by emissaries from the Lusitanians, a Hispanic tribe in the northwest of the peninsula. Having heard about his reputation, the Lusitanians sought to recruit him to ward off the Roman soldiers sent by Sulla. Believing that he might be able to force Rome to get rid of Sulla, Sertorius returned to Hispania and rallied a force of like-minded rebellious Romans. He met with initial success and even defeated the Roman governor of Hispania Ulterior (the Latin term for the Iberian Peninsula).

Sertorius then sent out his commander, Lucius Hirtuleius, who unseated the Sulla-appointed ruler in Hispania Citerior (the eastern coast of Iberia) and Hispania Tarraconensis (covered much of modern-day Spain). Because of the Sertorian threat, Sulla raised the status of Hispania to a proconsular province and sent over Quintus Caecilius Metellus Pius to act as a governor. Pius sent over his own commander, Domitius Calvinus, to seize Hispania Ulterior. He was blocked by fortifications built by Hirtuleius.

Hirtuleius and his men waged sporadic guerilla warfare. Little by little, the Roman forces moved inland, and Sertorius tried to fight them off. When Metellus Pius discovered this, he sent in his own armies. However, after many successful strikes by Sertorius, Metellus Pius called for reinforcements from Gallia Transalpina ("Transalpine Gaul"). They crossed the Pyrenees and waged battle with Hirtuleius but were defeated and forced to retreat to Gaul.

The Battle of Lauron

Rome then dispatched Gnaeus Pompeius Magnus, better known as Pompey, to seize control of the Spanish territories from Sertorius. In 76 BCE, Pompey marched along the Mediterranean coast of Hispania toward the town of Lauron. His troops were in need of supplies and sent out men to forage. Sertorius harassed them when they returned to join the troops, but then Sertorius sent in his heavy armored infantry divisions from the woods, which was followed by Sertorius's cavalry.

When Pompey discovered the foragers' predicament, he sent out a legion, but it was roundly defeated. Thankfully for him, he still had a sizeable force left.

Metellus Pius joined up with Pompey. They continued to work their way north through midland Hispania. Pompey then decided to circumvent the Romans and move toward northern Hispania.

The Battle of Italica

This battle, fought in 75 BCE between the forces of Hirtuleius and Metellus Pius, illustrates some of the Roman military's famous tactics. Metellus Pius attacked the weaker flanks first on either side and then encircled the Sertorian warriors in the center. It worked well, and Metellus Pius and the Romans won. Hirtuleius lost over 20,000 men.

Pamplona

In the winter of 75 CE, Pompey moved farther north of the Ebro and stopped at a town called Iruna, along the Arga River (known as the Runa River in contemporary history). He felt it was ideal for his encampment. The Arga River is a tributary of the Ebro in the modern-day Basque province of Álava. This was in the heart of the Vascone territory.

Pompey descended upon Iruna and called it "Pompaelo" (Pamplona), which is named after him. The city was in a strategic location, as it was close to the border of Gaul (France), La Rioja, and Aragon (the latter two areas are provinces of Hispania). All three of these areas were close to the Pyrenees and the border of Gaul. In ancient times, La Rioja was inhabited by the Autrigones and the Vascones. In addition, it was inhabited by the Berones, which was an ancient Celtic tribe.

When Pompey arrived, he immediately had his forces build heavy stone walls around the city. Those stone walls have been modified and rebuilt many times throughout history. The remnants of these walls still stand today. They were sometimes extended to enclose protected settlements belonging to the Romans and to other ethnic groups later on.

Fractures

Divisive elements erupted between the Iberians and the Roman Sertorian forces. The Romans were abusive of the Iberians, which, of course, kindled discontent. In fact, Sertorius himself was becoming paranoid, though that was probably for a justifiable reason. Taking advantage of the friction that had developed between the Iberians and the Roman troops under Sertorius, Metellus Pius made an offer. Any Roman who betrayed Sertorius would receive a reward of 100 silver talents and 20,000 acres of land. In 73 BCE, one of Sertorius's Roman commanders, Marcus Perperna Vento, organized some conspirators, and they murdered Sertorius.

Perperna attempted to regain the support of the Sertorians, but Pompey laid a trap for him. Pompey used the old tactic of the feigned retreat. He gathered up ten cohorts and hastily pulled back in the midst of fighting. As soon as Perperna and his forces rushed forward to confront them, Pompey's men suddenly turned heel and surprised them. It was a massacre.

Pompey returned with a vengeance, and he eventually defeated the Sertorian forces in southern Spain. The Vascones then returned to their native land. The ancient chronicler Livy indicates that little Romanization of the Basque territories occurred during the Roman occupation because Vasconia was so mountainous. Therefore, the Vascones and other Basque tribes were relatively free from Roman intrusion and control. Being mercenary soldiers rather than Roman subjects was to their advantage.

Roman Expansion under Crassus

In 58 BCE, the general Publius Licinius Crassus conquered some of the Aquitanian tribes to the north and east of Pamplona. Today, that Aquitanian territory is now the Basque Autonomous Community of Navarre. The Sotiates, a Gallic-Aquitani tribe, fought poorly in the battles against Crassus. This was because they left their rear weak, which resulted in a Roman victory. According to Caesar in his book, *Commentaries on the Gallic Wars*, "At last, after heavy casualties, a large number of the enemy fled from the field. A large number of them were slain."

Julius Caesar helped Crassus expand Roman territory and went up against Vercingetorix, the chieftain from the Arverni tribe of Gaul. He united a number of Gallic tribes to rebel against the Romans. His forces engaged Caesar at the Battle of Gergovia in 52 BCE. Vercingetorix won, but he was subsequently defeated by the Romans at Alesia in the same year.

It is interesting to note that Caesar made a clear distinction between the language of the Aquitanians and that of the Gauls. The Aquitanians spoke a form of "proto-Basque," the precursor of the Basque language, while the Gauls spoke a Celtic language.

The Cantabrian Wars

In 29 BCE, the Romans invaded the mountainous area inhabited by the Astures and the Cantabrians. For a portion of the wars, the Astur general was Gausón, while the Cantabrian commander was Corocotta. Cantabria was located along the northern coast of Hispania. The ancient historian Lucius Flores wrote that it was "that part which adjoins the cliffs where the Pyrenees end and is washed by the nearer waters of the ocean."

The Roman army would eventually be overseen by the emperor himself, Caesar Augustus. A victory over the Astures would shine a spotlight on Augustus's reign, as the Astures were noted for their ferocity and skill in using light armaments. This neighboring Basque tribe also used a special breed of horse called the Asturcón, named after the Astures. It is a short, stocky horse, and it was first described by the ancient historian Pliny the Elder. The horse is still bred today.

At that time, Cantabria was an independent region occupied by the Celtic Iberians (Celtiberians), and the Astures lived in a territory just to the west of them. The Astures and the Cantabrians agreed to cooperate so they could fight off the Romans. In 26 BCE, Augustus Caesar set up his encampment at Segisama (modern-day Sasamon, Spain), just to the east of Cantabria, with about 70,000 men. He split up his forces into three divisions, which the Cantabrians and Astures did as well.

The Siege of Aracillum

In 25 BCE, the Romans stormed up the Cantabrian Mountains with about 25,000 men and moved toward the town of Aracillum. The Cantabrians had an equal number of warriors. The Cantabrians had a hill fort there with about twelve miles of walls, battlements, and trenches. The Roman forces under Augustus Caesar and Gaius Antistius Vetus placed the Cantabrian fort under siege. Although the Cantabrians were able to hold up for quite some time, they eventually ran out of supplies. This was a distinct Roman victory.

The Cantabrians avoided being taken prisoner by committing suicide. In fact, this was the custom of both the Cantabrians and the Astures. They used a poison made from yew trees.

The Battle of Vellica

During the same year, the Cantabrians drew Augustus Caesar and his forces, which numbered a little over 5,000 warriors, out on the plain of Mave. Normally, when the Cantabrians had to fight in an open area, they preferred to set up their battlefield so as to situate a natural border against the enemies' backs. The Romans thought that maneuver was clever and gave it the name *circulus cantabricus,* meaning "Cantabrian circle." In the case of Vellica, it wasn't going to work.

Although they could have used their hill fortress as a base of operations, the Cantabrians didn't have enough supplies to defend the fort. It may have invited a siege they couldn't withstand. Despite the Cantabrians trying to think logically about the battle, the Romans handily won and moved westward toward the land of the Astures.

Battle near the Astura River

In the spring, three Roman legions under Augustus Caesar prepared to attack the land of the Astures. According to the ancient scholars, the Astur army descended the snow-capped mountains in droves. The first phase consisted of a series of guerilla-style attacks. The Astures then headed toward their fortified town of Lancia. Unfortunately, one division of the Astures betrayed their fellow warriors and gave Augustus Caesar an advance warning about the fortifications in Lancia.

The Romans moved upon Lancia and placed the town under siege. Although the ancient records are unclear, the Astur commander Gausón was either captured and executed at Lancia or died there during the siege.

Battle at Mons Medullius

Following that, the Astur army took refuge at Mons Medullius. The Romans dug a huge ditch (eighteen miles long!) and a moat alongside the mountain to prevent the Astures from escaping. Once they realized they were unable to repel the Romans, the Astures began committing suicide. According to the ancient historian Florus, "The barbarians, seeing that their last hour had come, vied with one another in hastening their own deaths in the midst of a banquet by fire and the sword and a poison commonly extracted from the yew tree."

Afterward, the Romans stationed two legions there to monitor those who remained. Archaeologists have since unearthed a well-preserved bust of Caesar Augustus in Zaragoza, a province in Tarazona, Spain.

Hispania was then divided by Caesar Augustus's general, Marcus Vipsanius Agrippa, into Lusitania, Baetica, Cantabria, and the Basque Country.

Later Roman Involvement

The Romans tended to colonize limited areas in the regions along the northern shore of Hispania after that, and there is little written history about their relations with the Basques in the Pyrenees region. Romans allowed the Basques to continue their lives as they did before, except for some limited activity on the northern coast of Hispania, which had access to the Bay of Biscay and the Celtic Sea just north of there. Most Roman interests lay in southern Hispania along the Mediterranean Sea.

Throughout ancient history, it was repeatedly said in the texts that the Basques were never entirely conquered by the Romans.

During the reign of Emperor Diocletian (284–305 CE), the Basque Country was a portion of what he called "Novempopulania," also known as "Aquitania Tertia." There was an admixture of peoples in that area, as some were of Hispanic origin, some of Basque origin, and others of French origin.

The northern areas of the Basque Country had silver mines, which were used to produce the coinage to pay the Roman troops. Archaeologists in the Basque Country have unearthed a number of these coins. They are inscribed with the word "IMON," which stood for "Barcunes," the Roman term for "Vascones." Those coins were made until 45 CE.

In 409 CE, the Vascone forces aided the Romans in fighting the Germanic barbarians— the Alans, the Suebi, and the Vandals—who had started to infiltrate the Roman Empire. In 418 CE, the Visigoths invaded. The Romans became overwhelmed by these tribes, and they drew up a treaty with the Visigoths. In exchange for driving the Alans, Suebi, and the Vandals out of Hispania, the Roman Empire awarded the Visigoths with huge segments of land in northeastern, eastern, and southeastern Hispania that they could settle.

Although there wasn't heavy colonization in the land of the Basques, there are many historic stone buildings that feature the Romanesque style of domes and gently tapered arches with hundreds of carved figures.

In 476 CE, the Western Roman Empire collapsed, and there was a scramble for the possession of the regions in the area near the Pyrenees.

Chapter 4 – Rule under Dukes, Counts, and Kings

Early Middle Age Feudal States

During the Middle Ages, the country of the Basques was generally referred to as Vasconia, after the name of its most prominent tribe. It was wedged between the Garonne River in current-day southwestern France and the Ebro River in northeastern Spain. The Ebro River runs through the Basque territory.

In 481, the Visigoths annexed some surrounding Basque areas, but they never fully conquered the entire Basque Country, which was larger back then than it is today. In 500 CE, the Visigoths controlled the tribal regions of northern Spain, southwestern Aquitaine except for the Basque Country in the northeast, and Cantabria, which was just west of there.

Evolution of the Three Duchies

The borders of today's Basque region were deeply affected by the events of the 6th century and into the Middle Ages. The borders of Francia and Hispania kept fluctuating, as Francia and the Visigoths struggled with each other.

In 507 CE, Aquitaine was still known by the Caesarian term "Gallia Aquitania." During the same year, the first king of the Franks was Clovis I. He started what was called the Merovingian dynasty. Clovis and his descendants kept dividing Gaul into smaller areas, creating instability. At that time, the Visigoths encroached at the southwestern borders of Gaul in the Basque territory.

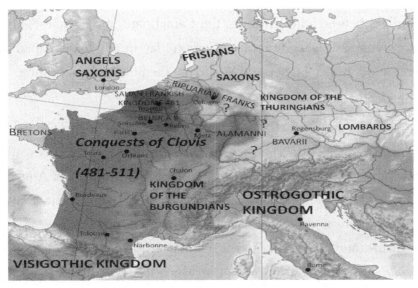

Basque territories showing the encroachments of the Visigoths and Franks
Altaileopard, CC BY-SA 3.0 <https://creativecommons.org/licenses/by-sa/3.0>, via Wikimedia Commons https://commons.wikimedia.org/wiki/File:Conquests_of_Clovis.png

Some smaller Gothic tribes lived in Cantabria and Vasconia. In 574 CE, King Liuvigild of the Visigoths marched against the Gothic tribes, the Cantabrians, and the Basques, invading and annexing two of the main Cantabrian towns that lay along the coast of the Bay of Biscay.

The Duchy of Cantabria

In the same year—574 CE—King Liuvigild created the Duchy of Cantabria after massacring the inhabitants. When he created Cantabria, Liuvigild absorbed some territories from the Vascones, but the Astures to the west continued to rebel. He used Cantabria as a buffer zone between the land of the Astures, which was just west of there, and the Duchy of Vasconia, which came to be called the Duchy of Gascony.

The Duchy of Gascony

In 629 CE, one of Clovis's successors, Charibert II, quelled the rebellious Basques. He had control of Aquitaine and Gascony by virtue of his marriage to Gisela, the heiress of Gascony.

Conflicts between the Visigoths, the Cantabrians, the Basques, and the Franks continued. Geographically, Gascony lay in an elbow-shaped area between modern-day France and Spain, but the borders kept shifting.

The Duchy of Aquitaine

In 602 CE, the Duchy of Aquitaine was established. In 660, Felix of Aquitaine was placed in charge of the areas within the Pyrenees, which included both the Duchy of Gascony and parts of the Duchy of Aquitaine. The Franks ruled in name only at this point, as the Duchy of Gascony was the true power in the region. Felix befriended the Basques and the Aquitanians, and he reached an agreement with them by making them *foederati*. This was an arrangement in which the overlord exchanged his protection and allegiance for military services against an enemy. At that time, the Aquitanians were permitted a degree of autonomy within Francia.

The *foederati* agreement was exercised by a later successor of Felix, Odo the Great. He became the duke of Aquitaine in 700 CE under the Frankish Merovingian dynasty. In the Battle of Toulouse in 721 CE, the Basques fended off the Saracens (Muslims) of the Umayyad dynasty, who were led by Abdul al-Rahman al-Ghafiqi. That earned Odo the epithet "the Great." Despite that title, Odo did lose possession of the historical Basque province of Sobrarbe in 724 CE. Today, that territory is part of Aragon in Spain.

When the Muslim threat accelerated, the famous Frankish leader Charles "The Hammer" Martel swung through Aquitaine, joined up with Odo the Great, and confronted the Muslims at Tours in 732 CE. Al-Ghafiqi was killed, and his army dispersed. The Battle of Tours was a Frankish/Aquitanian victory, and it is historically significant, as it kept the Muslims out of Gaul. It is interesting to note that the Muslims underplayed the role of that victory in their histories.

However, the Western world saw it as a triumph of Christianity over Islam. In truth, it had only occurred in Francia. That arrangement continued under Odo's son and successor, Hunald I, Duke of Aquitaine.

Hunald was succeeded by his son, Waiofer (also spelled as Waiofar or Waifer), in 745. In the meantime, Charles Martel and the Frankish leaders were anxious to unite all of these duchies under a single monarchy. After the death of Charles Martel, his sons, Carloman and Pepin the Short, schemed to wrench the Duchy of Aquitaine away from Waiofer. Pepin asked Carloman to help him obtain Aquitaine. Carloman refused, so Pepin himself rallied an army to defeat Waiofer.

When Waiofer wanted to negotiate peace, Pepin ignored him, saying he had confiscated Church lands to which he had no right, and marched to Aquitaine. Waiofer then recruited some of his own French supporters, along with the Basque tribes. According to a contemporary historical source, *The Chronicle of Fredegar*, in 765 CE, Waiofer went up against Pepin "with a great army and many Vascones [Gascons] from across the Garonne, who in antiquity were called Vaceti [Basques]."

At that point, Pepin seized many of the territories of Aquitaine, devastated the vineyards, and burnt the villas he encountered. In 766 CE, Waiofer's own men deserted him. However, the unrest continued. Waiofer's family was captured and executed. Pepin suggested to Waiofer's own men that they kill him, which they did in 768 CE. Pepin also died in 768, but before doing so, he left the task of dealing with the remnants of the rebellion to his two sons, Charles I, later known as Charlemagne, and Carloman I. Although Charlemagne asked for Carloman's help, none was forthcoming, but he managed quite well without it. Charlemagne marched his army in and took over the rest of Aquitaine. The son of Waiofer, Hunald II, had taken refuge in Gascony and was under the protection of Lupus, Duke of Gascony. Charlemagne demanded that Lupus end that protection. Terrified of the mighty Charlemagne, Lupus seized Hunald II along with his wife and handed them over to Charlemagne. He then paid homage to Charlemagne.

Autonomy was important to the Aquitanians, but it was lost in 769 CE, as the province yielded to Frankish suzerainty.

Charlemagne

In late 771, Carloman I died, and the kingdom of Francia came under the sole rule of his brother, Charlemagne. Charlemagne then assigned the Duchy of Aquitaine and the Duchy of Gascony to his son, Louis. There were numerous rebellions in Gascony due in no small part to the resurrected unrest by the Basques, who resented Frank domination, and by the nearby Muslim dynasty of Banu Qasi. Their territory lay just south of Gascony in the upper Ebro River valley. The Banu Qasi was from the Muwallad dynasty, who were of mixed ancestry but had married into the Muslims or were under their influence. The Muwallads were a part of the Umayyad Emirate at Córdoba.

Pamplona was the capital city of the Duchy of Gascony, and it was inhabited by the Basques and Muslims. There was some strife there, but a moderate degree of tolerance was practiced within Pamplona between the Muslims and the Basques. That was due to the efforts of Charlemagne's predecessor, Pepin the Short. Pepin had made a pact with the Muslims to allow Christianity in Pamplona as long as the Christians paid the jizya, a special tax paid to the Emirate of Córdoba. The Emirate of Córdoba was the Muslim administration that controlled most of Spain.

Charlemagne's Disaster

In order to enforce Christianity upon these people, Charlemagne first tore down the walls of Pamplona and then nearly destroyed the city. Both Christian and Muslim Basques were outraged and planned revenge. Religion wasn't an issue for the Basques; however, the occupation of their territory was.

In an effort to expand his Frankish empire into Muslim Spain, Charlemagne attacked Zuberoa in 778 CE. Zuberoa is the historical Basque province of Soule. It was (and is) a Basque province. The Muslims had the Basques, who had been forcefully converted to Christianity, as their allies. Charlemagne met up with the Basques at the treacherous Roncevaux Pass. This was a narrow mountain path with an elevation of 3,500 feet. The Basques, who were veteran mountain fighters, separated the rearguard of the Frankish forces along with their supplies. According to the *Annales regni Francorum* (the *Royal Frankish Annals*), "The Franks were superior to the Vascones [Basques] both in armament and in courage, but the roughness of the terrain and the difference in the style of combat made them [the Franks] generally weaker."

The rearguard that had been left behind earlier in the battle were slaughtered "to the last man," at least according to later medieval historians. Charlemagne's well-known fighter, Roland, also died during this military disaster. This great battle was memorialized in the poem *The Song of Roland*. It laments France's loss, spoken as if through the mouth of Roland: "O land of France, O blissful pleasant land, today laid desolate by such cruel waste! Brave French, I see you die on my account, and I unable to protect your lives." Scholars believe it was written by the French-Norman poet Turold between 1040 and 1115.

An anonymous Basque poet wrote of the same battle from the Basque point of view: "What were they in our hills, these Northern men? Why come they here to our quiet land? God made the hills intending for none should pass...Streams of red blood! Quivers among the mangled flesh! Oh! What a sea of blood! What shattered bones!" And he later added the verse that identified the battle with Roland at Roncevaux Pass: "Fly, Charlemagne, red cloak and raven plumes! Lies thy stout nephew, Roland, stark in death; for him his brilliant courage naught avails." This poem was found in the year 1794 in a convent in Fuentarrabía (often known as Hondarribia in English) in the Basque Country.

Charlemagne endured a huge setback at his defeat at Roncevaux Pass, as he had intended to proceed unimpaired through the rest of Hispania, which was mostly controlled by the Muslim Emirate of Córdoba.

In the 8th century, the Franks struggled against the Muslim invaders, who were intent upon conquering all of current-day Spain. The relationship between the Basques and the Muslims was a rocky one, and the two parties vacillated between peace and war. During that time, a segment of the Basque population, especially those who lived in the Ebro River Valley, adopted a form of Islam. The Basques who lived in the northern area of the Ebro Valley, however, were not converted, and they continued to practice Christianity or their ancient pagan religion. Although the Franks had control, their efforts were short-lived. In 812, the Franks under Louis the Pious once again fought against the Emirate of Córdoba.

In 816 CE, at the Battle of Pancorbo, the Basque king, Velasco the Basque, had the support of the Franks and also received aid from the Kingdom of Asturias, which was founded by the Visigoths in 718. All of them went up against Abd al-Karim ibn Abd al-Wahid at Pancorbo, an area full of fords, rivers, ravines, and mountain passes through the Pyrenees. The battle raged for thirteen days. The rivers were loaded up with logs, making them impossible to navigate. When the Christian Basque troops tried to cross the river, they were massacred by the Muslims. Many others died falling off the steep cliffs. The Muslims won, but the Basques staged more revolts, which were mostly directed against their Frankish overlords.

After this fateful battle, the Basque leader, Íñigo Arista, fostered the rebuilding of the city and the fortifications at Pamplona, starting in 790 CE.

Chapter 5 – The Middle Ages

Navarre

In 824 CE, Íñigo Arista was elected as the king of Pamplona, partially due to his deeds in the Battle of Pancorbo. He was Christian, but his half-brother, Musa ibn Musa of the Banu Qasi, was Muslim and permitted Arista to control the city of Pamplona as long as they paid the jizya, the taxes charged to non-Muslims. There were occasional rebellions there between Christian and Muslim forces, but Íñigo's objective was to establish a Basque state that wouldn't be subservient to the domination of the Emirate of Córdoba or the Franks. That state would be the Kingdom of Navarre.

After Íñigo died in 851, his remains were buried in the Romanesque-style monastery of Leyre in what is now San Salvador, Navarre.

His half-brother, Musa ibn Musa, took over Navarre, and Arista's son, García Íñiguez I, was made the king of Pamplona. In Navarre, many of the nobles defected to the Emirate of Córdoba. Absent of a popular power base, Musa also defected as well. During 851, Musa had to deal with an insurrection by the Basques. The Basques allied themselves with the Kingdom of Asturias but were defeated at the Battle of Albelda. Musa then threw the Basque and Asturian leaders into a dungeon.

By 854 CE, Musa took control of the provinces of Zaragoza, Huesca, Tudela, and Toledo. He was then referred to as the "Third King of Hispania."

Later, possibly in 860, another battle was waged against the Muslims by the Basque king of Pamplona, García Íñiguez, and King Ordoño I of Asturias. It was said the Muslims were defeated at the Battle of Monte Laturce and forced to flee. Over time, facts surrounding that battle were adapted as a backdrop for the legendary battle called the Battle of Clavijo. It is steeped in an old Christian legend and states that James, Jesus Christ's apostle, appeared at Clavijo and led the Christians to victory.

After García passed away, the area was restive, as his eldest son and successor, Fortún Garcés, was weak. Before the end of Fortún's reign, Sancho Garcés received the aid of Alfonso III of the Asturians and assumed control in 905 CE, ending the Íñiguez dynasty.

Sancho was strictly anti-Muslim and worked to expel the Emirate of Córdoba from the Kingdom of Navarre. In 911 CE, a former ally of his, Galindo Aznárez II, allied himself with two Muslim lords, Abd Allah ibn Lubb and Muhammad al-Tawil. They attacked Sancho but were defeated. Muhammad fled, and it is assumed that ibn Lubb fled with him. Galindo was forced to become a vassal. Little by little, the Muslim territories in that area were shrinking.

In 918, Sancho allied with Ordoño II of León to flush out the Muslims from the Upper March, which lay in the Ebro Valley. They conquered the towns of Calahorra, Arnedo, and Viguera from the Banu Quasi. Though they failed to capture the municipality of Valtierra, they did burn down the mosque there. The son of Muhammad al-Tawil, Amrus ibn Muhammad, wanted to set up his own private kingdom, so Sancho and his allies joined together to oust the Banu Qasi-held territory of Monzón. This allowed Sancho to expand his dominion into Lower Navarre.

The Battle of Calatañazor

In 1002, more Muslims entered Hispania. They were called the "Saracens" by medieval historians, as they lacked detailed information about the various caliphates in the Arab world. The Christian forces fought under Alfonso V of León, a Spanish province; Sancho III of Navarre; and Count Sancho García of Castile. The Muslims were led by Almanzor. He may not have held the title of a ruler, but he was definitely the one with the power in the Umayyad Caliphate of Córdoba, the ruling body that had replaced the former Emirate of Córdoba.

The Battle of Calatañazor was a major battle in the campaign by the Christians to expel the Muslims out of the province of Castile in Spain. This day-long battle occurred in the province of Calatañazor, which straddled both Castile and León. In preparation for this battle, Almanzor recruited troops from North Africa. There were thousands of troops who participated. In the end, Almanzor and his forces were defeated. Almanzor was wounded, but history indicates that he continued to wage war against the Christians in Spain. Eventually, he came upon a castle fortress manned by Christian warriors. There, he was defeated. Almanzor's health declined due to the wounds he incurred at Calatañazor, and he became more debilitated. As he lay dying, he said to his son, "This appears to me the first sign of the decadence that awaits the empire." According to a local legend, a mysterious fisherman appeared in another town and said, "In Calatañazor, Almanzor lost the drum." This was believed to be the lament of the devil when his demons failed to prevail over the forces of good.

Sancho Garcés III: Sancho the Great

During the 9th century, the Kingdom of Navarre grew in prestige and importance. In Basque history, Sancho Garcés III is featured as one of the country's greatest unifiers and one of its most important kings, which is why he inherited his nickname "the Great." In 1004, he was the king of Pamplona. Through marriage, he came to rule the County of Castile, along with the feudal states of Álava and Monzón.

Under Sancho's successors, the Kingdom of Navarre was divided into Castile, Pamplona, and the Basque provinces of Ribagorza, Sobrarbe, and the new province of Aragon. These areas had expanded under Sancho Garcés to include not only the lowlands but also the urban centers. Because of that, the Basques intermingled with the French, causing a predominance of French- and Spanish-speaking people. Due to this, the Basque language became the language of the minority. This is why some of the regions of the Basque Country today speak only *Euskara*, while other regions speak a mixture of Basque, Spanish, and French.

García Sánchez III

Sancho III made arrangements with his sons before his death in terms of their inheritances. García III was the eldest son of Sancho III, and as such, he was to inherit the kingship of Navarre (Pamplona) and would have control of Álava and Gipuzkoa. His brother, Ferdinand I, was to have control over part of the County of Castile, while García III would oversee the other, larger portion of Castile. Ramiro I received the County of Aragon, and Gonzalo was given the rulership over the Basque territories of Sobrarbe and Ribagorza.

After Gonzalo died unexpectedly in 1043, Ramiro was awarded Aragon, Sobrarbe, and Ribagorza. At that time, Ribagorza and Sobrarbe were assimilated into the Spanish province of Aragon. Upon Ramiro's death, his son, Sancho Ramírez, had control of Navarre (Pamplona) and

Aragon. Sancho Ramírez then called himself "King of the Aragonese and Pamplonese." He was the first to proclaim himself King of Aragon.

"Emperor" Ferdinand

In 1037, García Sánchez III and Ferdinand I went to war with the Kingdom of León, a Spanish territory just west of Pamplona. By that time, it included much of the territory once belonging to the Kingdom of Asturias. García and Ferdinand defeated King Bermudo III of León, who was killed in the battle. Ferdinand then became the king of León, as well as the count of Castile. However, in time, the brothers argued about the distribution of the lands of León, Castile, and Pamplona. In 1054, Ferdinand battled his brother at the ancient mountains near Atapuerca, and García was killed.

García Sánchez's son, Sancho, was the legitimate heir of the estate, as inheritances were passed along to the direct descendants. Sancho was only fourteen in 1054, so his mother, Stephanie, was the regent. Sancho was crowned king of Pamplona and became Sancho Garcés IV immediately after his father's death.

Ferdinand was said to have called himself "emperor," basing that on the charters of Aragon drawn up in 1056, which says Ferdinand was the "emperor in León and in Castile." Ferdinand's consort was Queen Sancha, the sister of deceased King Bermudo III of León, which may have been interpreted as strengthening Ferdinand's claim.

Ferdinand took advantage of Sancho and reduced Navarre (Pamplona) to the status of a vassal state. Ferdinand was ambitious. He captured Zaragoza in 1060 CE, which, at that time, was under Muslim control. The emir was then made to pay tribute to Ferdinand.

Ferdinand craved the territory of Toledo, so he attacked its two neighboring cities, Talamanca and Alcalá de Henares, and conquered them. The emir of Toledo, Yahya ibn Ismail al-Mamun, wanted to avoid the destruction of Toledo, so he submitted himself to Ferdinand.

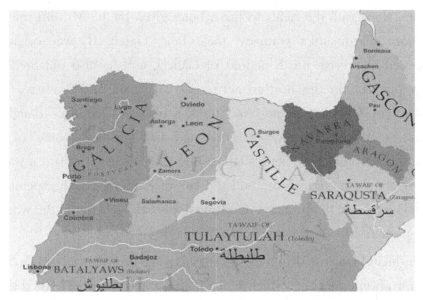

The Iberian Peninsula with its 11th-century Provinces and those of Francia
The original uploader was Alexandre Vigo at Galician Wikipedia., CC BY-SA 3.0
<http://creativecommons.org/licenses/by-sa/3.0/>, via Wikimedia Commons
https://commons.wikimedia.org/wiki/File:Europe-south-west-kingdoms.png

In 1063, Ferdinand continued to expand his territories in Spain and raided the Muslim states of Badajoz and Seville. He raided them as a scare tactic, and the Muslim rulers agreed to pay tribute to him to avoid future raids. Although it was a form of extortion, this was a common practice in those days.

In 1065, Ferdinand invaded Valencia. Before Ferdinand could reach the heart of the territory, Emir Abd al-Malik al-Muzaffar submitted to him, agreeing to pay tribute.

The Death of Ferdinand

Like his father, Ferdinand decided to make arrangements for the inheritances of his children before he died.

Even though Alfonso VI wasn't his eldest son, Ferdinand chose to bequeath the Kingdom of León to him. Sancho II, also known as Sancho "the Strong," who was the eldest, received Pamplona and the Kingdom of Castile, along with the rights to the tributes given by the Muslim ruler of Zaragoza. Ferdinand's youngest male heir, García II, was originally supposed to receive the Kingdom of Galicia, and he also obtained the lands that lay on the northwestern coast of Spain and Navarre. The territory of Galicia was unstable until Ferdinand's younger daughter, Elvira, was given the city of Toro and half of the income of the monasteries within Ferdinand's lands. His other daughter, Urraca, was to receive the monastic income and the city of Zamora. Arrangements for the income from the monastic lands was only valid as long as the women were unmarried.

Ferdinand became deathly ill during his siege of Valencia and decided to return home to León, which he had confiscated earlier. He died there in 1065.

El Cid and Sancho II

Sancho II decided to recruit Rodrigo Díaz de Vivar, an accomplished knight, to help him challenge Alfonso for possession of León. Rodrigo was also called El Cid by the Muslim Moors, whom he had dealings with as part of his service to the kings and nobles in Spain.

El Cid helped Sancho II defeat Alfonso at the Battle of Golpejera in 1072. After that, Alfonso was arrested. For some reason, Sancho II decided to spare his brother. Alfonso was exiled to the city of Toledo, which was in the hands of a Muslim king. Sancho II then became the king of León and Castile.

El Cid also helped Sancho lay siege to the city of Zamora, which was held by his sister Urraca. In a strange twist of fate, a nobleman by the name of Vellido Adolfo was hired to assassinate Sancho II. He lured Sancho into meeting with him privately, saying that he knew of a weakness in the Castle of Zamora. When Sancho rounded the corner of the castle,

Vellido stabbed him. El Cid gave chase, but Vellido slipped out of the city through a gateway and vanished. Today, that gateway is called *Portillo del Traidor* or, in English, "Gateway of the Traitor."

After his father's murder, Sancho IV inherited the rights to Pamplona. Sancho was also crowned as the king of Pamplona (Navarre). Likewise, he was the count of Álava, Bureba, Gipuzkoa, Biscay, and Alta Rioja. However, in 1076, he was assassinated by his jealous siblings at a promontory in Navarre.

With the death of Sancho IV, Alfonso VI became the king of León and Castile, and he also gained Sancho IV's territories of Navarre, Álava, Bureba, Gipuzkoa, Biscay, and Alta Rioja. An issue arose regarding the kingship of Navarre. To resolve the crisis, it was decided that Navarre would be divided between Alfonso VI and Sancho V Ramírez. In the end, part of Navarre was in Castile, and the other portion was in Aragon.

Civil War

Alfonso VI had no male heirs, so he tried to arrange for a successor. He legitimatized his mistress, Zaida, in order to have a male heir. She was a Muslim princess, and they had a son together. Zaida converted to Catholicism and was renamed "Isabel." In 1103, Alfonso met with his councilors and named his only son, Sancho Alfónsez, as his heir presumptive. Alfonso's carefully laid succession plan went awry when Sancho went to war against the Muslim Almoravids of Toledo, for he lost the Battle of Uclés in 1107. After the battle, Sancho was on the run. He was killed by villagers in 1108.

Alfonso VI was desperate. Not wanting his lands to fall into the hands of his rivals, Alfonso made his widowed daughter, Urraca, the heir presumptive. To seal her right to the throne, the Leonese and Castilian nobles insisted she marry. Alfonso objected to the suitors they presented, as they could become fierce rivals. He selected King Alfonso I of Aragon around 1109. Alfonso I was the son of Sancho V Ramírez, making Urraca and Alfonso second cousins. That way, everything stayed "within the family," so to speak. However, that became a problem later on.

Alfonso the "Battler" and a Woman's Wiles

Alfonso was noted for his military prowess, and he was said to have won "twenty-nine" battles. He also fought alongside El Cid in Valencia. For his efforts, his father, Sancho V Ramírez, awarded him with the rulership of Ardennes, Luna, Bailo, and Biel.

Alfonso's marriage was performed for political reasons. Urraca's father, Alfonso VI, had caveats attached to their marriage contract. First of all, the contract indicated that if either party left the other without a mutual agreement, he or she would forfeit the support of their followers. Neither of them could leave the other because of their familiar relationship to each other or for fear of excommunication by the pope.

Furthermore, if Urraca gave birth to a male, that child would inherit both Alfonso's and Urraca's properties. In the case that Urraca had no male child, her properties would be bequeathed to her successors, not his. If Urraca died first, her properties would be awarded to her son by her prior marriage, Alfonso Raimúndez.

In 1110, Alfonso and Urraca separated. Alfonso had been a bachelor for many years, and it was said he preferred the company of men to women, though there's no indication this was true. It would seem, though, that he had difficulty relating to women, especially his ambitious wife.

Alfonso claimed total control of Castile, León, Toledo, and Aragon. In 1114, their marriage was annulled for reasons of consanguinity. Of course, that meant their marriage contract was null and void, but Alfonso still held on to his lands. Urraca was nearly as militaristic as her husband. She raised her own troops and marched against Alfonso. Her forces attacked Castile, but Alfonso, who was anxious to return to his conquests of the

Muslim lands in Spain, made a truce with Urraca.

Alfonso the "Battler"
https://commons.wikimedia.org/wiki/File:Estatua_de_Alfonso_I_de_Arag%C3%B3n.jpg

Urraca later became involved in a conflict with Bishop Diego Gelmírez of Galicia. The bishop had appointed a guardian, Pedro Fróilaz de Traba, for Urraca's underage son, Alfonso Raimúndez. De Trada was a highly politicized figure in Galicia and detested Urraca and her high-handed ways. In 1121, Urraca made the colossal error of arresting the bishop in retaliation for the selection of de Traba. When threatened with excommunication by Pope Callixtus II, Urraca immediately made amends. Otherwise, she would have lost control of all her holdings.

Urraca died in 1126, and her son and heir, Alfonso VII (Alfonso Raimúndez), started a campaign to regain all of the territories that had been lost to Alfonso the Battler.

Peace of Támara

In 1127, Alfonso I the Battler made an agreement with the younger Alfonso to determine the possessions within Castile and Aragon. They agreed Alfonso I would be the ruler of Biscay, Gipuzkoa, Belorado, Soria, Buerba, San Esteban de Gormaz, and Alta Rioja.

By doing this, they reverted the border of Castile to its original borders of 1054. In return, Alfonso I recognized Alfonso VII as the king of Castile.

Battle of Fraga

In 1134, Alfonso I the Battler sent his forces from Aragon and the neighboring city of Barcelona to conquer the Muslim-held areas in the lowlands leading to the Ebro River Valley. The Muslim forces, which numbered 2,700 knights, besieged the town of Fraga in Aragon. Alfonso clashed with the cavalry sent by the emir of Murcia when they arrived on the scene. The battle dragged on. When the emir of Córdoba sent in more forces, they decimated Alfonso's troops. The beaten Alfonso then gathered up the survivors and fled to a district of Zaragoza. Alfonso I died of his wounds several days later.

The Crisis over Navarre and Castile

After the deaths of Alfonso I and Urraca, there was a succession crisis. For about half a century, Navarre had been divided between Castile and Aragon. After Alfonso I died, he left his properties to the Knights Templar, the Hospitallers, and the Knights of the Holy Sepulchre. All three of these were semi-religious orders. The nobility of Aragon objected to this, though. In order to resolve the issue, they looked back at the line of succession. A convocation of nobles decided that Ramiro II, Alfonso I's brother The Navarrese nobles sought out García Ramírez, who was the great-grandson of Sancho III. García Ramírez was also known as García the Restorer because he restored independence to Navarre, which had been joined to Aragon for decades.

The issue of the other Basque districts that had been seized by Alfonso I the Battler, and subsequently by his son, Alfonso VII, wasn't yet resolved. García Ramírez fought with Castile over its western lands. Alfonso VII and García made a pact in which the historic Basque districts of Álava, Biscay, Gipuzkoa, and Alta Rioja would be returned. However, Alfonso never kept the agreement. Regardless, Alfonso continued to let Navarre retain much of its self-government. He did that in order to obtain their favor. The viceroys of the towns swore to uphold their traditional charters, and in exchange, Navarre agreed to cede La Rioja to Castile.

However, the successive kings of Castile worked on granting the people in those territories, including Navarre, a high level of self-government. In fact, other towns and districts in Castile gained a limited state of autonomy under charters later called *fueros*. When trade routes were more firmly established, towns were able to secure charters by which they could operate as semi-independent provinces. Castile permitted those provinces to pass their own laws and keep their own customs.

"Tall" Sancho

The son of Sancho VI (the son and successor of García Ramírez) and Sancha (the daughter of Alfonso VII of León and Castile) was Sancho VII. He became the king of Navarre in 1194. A forensic anthropologist recently discovered that Sancho VII was over seven feet tall, which must have made an impression on the people around him. In 1212, he joined forces with the neighboring Christian provinces to expel the Muslims. It was said that Sancho's Basque soldiers carried shields emblazoned with a star symbol, which represented the Sun of Death or possibly the Christian symbol of life and death.

Sancho's sisters were Berengaria and Blanche. Berengaria was married to Richard the Lionheart of England, and it was said that Sancho and the

English king were fairly close. Blanche died in 1229, and Berengaria passed in 1230. When Sancho died in 1234, he had no heirs. Since he had no siblings left to give the throne to, Navarre went to Blanche's son, Theobald IV, Count of Champagne. This transfer was supported by the Navarrese nobility.

King Theobald I of Navarre

In 1234, Count Theobald IV of Champagne became Theobald I, King of Navarre. Since he hailed from a foreign territory, he knew nothing about the Basques.

King Theobald came to understand that the Basques were unique and different from their Indo-European neighbors, and he developed the first written charters, or *fueros*, to promote smooth relations with the monarchy of Navarre and the Basque people. In 1238, he drew up the first *Fuero General de Navarra* ("General Charter of Navarre"). This charter defined the distribution of powers among the king, the courts, and the parliament (called the *Cortes*), which represented the people. The Basques maintained their customs and had a set of laws for themselves, but those laws were really common laws delivered orally throughout the ages. Theobald's direct successor, Theobald II, upheld the policies of his father. His son, Henry I, also confirmed the *fueros* of Navarre.

While there was a mix of languages spoken over the years in the Basque Country, *Euskara*, the traditional Basque language, was mainly spoken. In some of the areas, Spanish and French were also used. The Basques often called the non-Basque speaking population "Gascons," after the historical term "Vascones."

Chapter 6 – The Late Middle Ages

Autonomy/Home Rule in the French Basque Country

The representative assemblies, called the Juntas Generales, represented the Basque population in France, with its provinces of Labourd, Soule, and Lower Navarre. (Upper Navarre is located in Spain.)

Hostilities Build

In 1285, King Theobald's granddaughter, Joan I, became the queen of Navarre. She never visited Navarre and instead put it in the hands of French governors, who were very unpopular. Philip IV of France, Joan's wife, retained the kingdom of Navarre for France.

The throne of France and Navarre eventually fell into the hands of Philip V (in Navarre, he was known as Philip II). Some of the English holdings in France had been transferred to the royalty in England by virtue of marriage, which only helped to contribute to the friction between England and France. Philip V ruled Navarre from 1316 to 1322. He saw to it that women could not succeed to the throne, and he was succeeded by Charles IV, his brother (known as Charles I in Navarre).

Edward II, the king of England, was also the duke of Aquitaine and had territories in Gascony. He was expected to pay homage to King Charles IV. However, he delayed because of some conspiracies at home. In retribution, Charles IV confiscated some of Edward's lands. In order to resolve the situation, Edward appealed to Pope John XXII. The pope contacted Charles, who agreed to return some of the lands if Edward paid homage. Aware of the difficulties Edward had in England, the pope made arrangements for Edward's wife, Isabella, to serve as an ambassador. To maintain control, royal families frequently intermarried. As it so happened, Isabella was also Charles IV's sister.

Upon her arrival, Isabella and Charles made a truce. The truce specified that the French lands would be returned with the exception of a small portion of land called Agenais if Isabella's son, Prince Edward, would pay him homage on behalf of his father. After Prince Edward arrived, he paid homage, but Charles didn't return the Aquitaine properties. However, France could resume control of its other lands there.

That wasn't satisfactory. Isabella was a schemer who almost always got what she wanted. She was dubbed as the "She-Wolf" of France because of that. This time, she wanted the reacquisition of Aquitaine. Besides, she wanted to stay in France so she could pursue a relationship with Roger Mortimer, an exiled Englishman. Her son, Edward, was with her, so she decided to betroth him to Philippa, the daughter of a local count. Marriage with royals of another territory would come in handy for her scheme.

She then decided to invade England with a mercenary army. She had the powerful duke of Lancaster, with an entourage of bishops, present her husband, Edward II, with two options: 1) abdicate the throne in favor of his son, or 2) have his son disinherited (in which case the throne would go to an alternate candidate). Faced with that choice, Edward reluctantly abdicated.

When some of the notables in the kingdom saw these machinations, they tried to go to his rescue. Rapidly, Mortimer sequestered the miserable Edward II in Berkeley Castle. In 1327, he died. The timing seemed rather convenient, but no one could prove that any foul play was involved.

Charles IV died in 1328, but he had no male heirs. He was succeeded by his niece, Joan II of Navarre, and his cousin, Philip VI of Valois. Edward III of England was expected to return and pay homage to Philip. He did so, but he offended the French by failing to remove his crown at the ceremony.

Further friction occurred when France supported the Kingdom of Scotland in their resistance to England. For years, the English monarchs wanted to conquer Scotland. Once France gave its allegiance to Scotland, King Edward III knew he couldn't succeed in gaining control over the Scots.

Tensions grew between England and France. England had given refuge to Robert III of Artois, a devious English nobleman who fled France when charged with forgery. In 1336, France demanded his extradition, but England refused. Tensions between both countries were at a fever pitch.

Artois used this animosity to his own advantage. He grabbed the ear of young Edward III and reminded him that he had the right to claim the throne of France through his marriage to Philippa of Hainault. She was descended from Charles of Valois, the father of King Philip VI of France.

The Hundred Years' War

Because of his familial connections to the royalty of France, Edward III of England formally declared himself "King of France and the French royal arms" in 1340. In 1346, the English army under Edward III landed in Normandy, and it plowed a path of destruction across northern France.

In August of 1346, the two armies met at Crécy. They moved southward and reached the River Seine. The English longbowmen were Edward's most effective division. They wiped out the French forces they encountered and moved up toward Calais, along the northern coast of France.

Philip VI died in 1350, which was around the same time the Black Plague hit France and England. Troops, especially those of France, were decimated by the disease. Philip's successor, John II, continued the struggle.

In Poitiers, Edward III's son, Edward, better known as Edward the Black Prince of Wales, led his army from Gascony and continued plundering. With the aid of a Gascon noble, Jean III de Grailly, Prince Edward met up with King John II's army in 1356. John II was actually captured and taken prisoner, making France kingless. The French Dauphin, who was the heir presumptive, and England tried to negotiate a settlement. After several years, the Treaty of Brétigny was signed. A huge ransom was to be paid for the release of King John II, and Edward III renounced his claim on the French throne. Furthermore, John was required to send his younger son, Louis, Duke of Anjou, as a hostage. In exchange, France would cede Aquitaine to England. Louis of Anjou later escaped, and John II returned to England as a hostage. He felt dishonored by the actions of his son and wanted to keep to the terms that had been agreed upon. He died in prison (although it should be noted he lived fairly nicely for a prisoner and was treated with great respect) and was succeeded by Charles V.

In Spain, there was a dispute over the provinces of Castile and Aragon. That became an issue, as Charles V recruited allies from Castile. Thus, both England and France became embroiled in the Castilian Civil War.

The Castilian Civil War

In Spain, King Peter was the ruler of Castile and León. However, his half-brother, Henry of Trastámara, who lived in France at the time, laid claim to the throne. With the support of Charles V of France, Henry gathered an army of French soldiers. He also had help from the Black Prince of England and a soldier of fortune named Bertrand du Guesclin. In exchange for the Black Prince's aid, Henry of Trastámara agreed to help defray the costs of the battle. With their massive army, they attacked Peter. He was deposed and was forced to flee.

Henry of Trastámara then returned to Castile in 1368 to a rousing welcome. He was supported as the king of Castile by the local nobles.

However, Peter had not given up. In 1369, Peter of Castile again confronted Henry at the fortress of Montiel. Henry besieged the fort and prevailed. Henry's envoy, Bertrand du Guesclin, met Peter to discuss terms. Peter promised to pay Bertrand 200,000 gold coins and the towns of Soria, Atienza, and Almazan if he betrayed Henry of Trastámara. When Bertrand returned, he told Henry of the offer, using it to his advantage to get paid more by Henry, who, of course, wanted Peter gone. Bertrand then returned to Peter and led him to his tent, in which Henry was hiding. Henry didn't immediately recognize Peter, as they had not seen each other in a long time. When Peter identified himself, Henry attacked him with a knife, and Peter fell to the ground. Then Henry stabbed him numerous times and left him unburied for three days. Thus, Henry (now Henry II) became the king of Castile and León.

After the death of Charles V of France in 1380, Charles VI ascended to the throne. However, Charles was mentally ill, and the duke of Orléans and the duke of Burgundy descended into their own civil war. Duke John of Burgundy was killed in 1419.

England took advantage of the internal conflicts in France by stepping up their attacks under Henry V. In 1415, Henry crossed into Normandy. The French forces pursued him, but Henry defeated them at the Battle of Agincourt. The French were unprepared to go up against Henry's much larger force, and about 6,000 French soldiers were killed.

Philip, who became Duke of Burgundy after his father's death, wanted to put an end to the constant hostilities. He proposed that Henry V of England marry Charles VI's daughter, Catherine. That way, Catherine would be an heir to the French throne, and Henry could act as her regent. Upon the death of King Charles VI, the French crown would go to Henry's heirs. That would yield a dual monarchy—that of England and France. In 1420, this was agreed to in what is known as the Treaty of Troyes.

Catherine and Henry V gave birth to Henry VI in 1421. When both Charles VI and Henry V died in 1422, the treaty was essentially tossed out the window. Although the throne should have gone to Henry VI, Dauphin Charles of France claimed it as his own. He ran into many difficulties and soon found himself on the losing side of the war.

The famous Joan of Arc inspired the Dauphin not to give up hope. She herself led the French forces in the Battle of Orléans, which was a rousing success. After that, the Dauphin marched to Rheims, where he was crowned King Charles VII of France.

As one might expect, England didn't recognize this claim. In Compiégne, Joan was captured and sent to England for trial. She was convicted of heresy and was burned at the stake in 1431.

Joan of Arc's execution

https://commons.wikimedia.org/wiki/File:Stilke_Hermann_Anton_-_Joan_of_Arc%27s_Death_at_the_Stake.jpg

Despite this setback, France went on to win the war in 1453. Not much changed for the Basques, although if the English had won, things most certainly would have.

Spanish Conquest of Navarre

Two noble families, the Beaumonts and the Agramonts, fought over control of Navarre and created problems in the Basque Country. In 1484, the control of Navarre was hotly contested, as the French portion of it lay on the northern section of the Pyrenees, where the Beaumonts were established, and the southern portion lay on the southern section, which was in Spain, where the Agramonts lived. Disagreements between the Spanish and French nobles ensued over control of Navarre. King Ferdinand II, who controlled Aragon and Castile through his marriage to Queen Isabella I, wanted to claim all of Navarre as a Spanish territory.

In 1504, Queen Isabella died. Her successor was her daughter, Joanna. Joanna was often called Joanna the Mad because of her severe mental instability. Although she was the ruling monarch of Castile, she was placed in a royal convent at Tordesillas by her father, Ferdinand II of Aragon. Joanna had a son named Charles, but he wasn't of age, so Ferdinand was his regent.

In 1512, Ferdinand joined the "Holy League," which was formed by Pope Julius II, who named France as an enemy to the interests of the papacy. For Ferdinand, this was merely a way to justify attacking northern Navarre. In 1512, Ferdinand organized a Spanish military force in the Basque province of Gipuzkoa and attacked Navarre, conquering the fortifications there. Ferdinand's force was huge, and the Beaumonts had to retreat.

The Castilian troops, manned mostly by soldiers from Gipuzkoa, crossed the Pyrenees via its passes. Once they arrived, they confiscated or destroyed the buildings belonging to the Beaumont faction. Ferdinand and his forces marched to the walls of the capital city of Pamplona, where he insisted the inhabitants swear allegiance to him. Pamplona capitulated, and Ferdinand then stationed his troops throughout the area. Ferdinand further demanded that John III of Navarre swear allegiance to him and send his young heir apparent, Henry, to the Castilian court to be raised there. John III and his wife, Catherine, refused. Instead, they fled and sought refuge in the neighboring province of Béarn.

Ferdinand made many efforts to justify his right to assume control of Navarre by obtaining papal support. Ferdinand offered concessions and agreed to respect Navarrese laws. The status of Navarre shifted in 1512 when Ferdinand was appointed king of Navarre.

Two Navarrese Counterattacks

John III, the former king of Navarre, saw his chance to retake Navarre after the death of Ferdinand in January 1516. So, John organized a military force of mostly Vascone soldiers. They took a number of prisoners, including some members of the Agramont family. However, John III's military failed to gain total control of the French area of Navarre.

Spain was in an economic downturn at that time, and Francis I of France jumped at the opportunity to gain control of Navarre. However, he was not the only one. Henry II, the son of John III and Catherine, was living in exile in Béarn. He was the rightful heir to the Kingdom of Navarre, and he gathered an army of 12,000 Vascones and displaced Navarrese to fight for his rightful throne.

Ignatius Loyola and the Battle of Pamplona

Ignatius Loyola, the future founder of the Jesuits, was initially a military man. Ignatius, or Íñigo in the Basque language, was born in the Basque province of Gipuzkoa. He was an expert swordsman and somewhat violent in his youth. He even had duels with other men, sometimes over issues related to his Catholic beliefs.

In 1521, Ignatius served as the Castilian military governor of Pamplona, the capital of Navarre. His commander, Antonio Manrique de Lara, 2nd Duke of Nájera, and his forces were away from Pamplona, fighting a local rebellion, when the French invaded. Ignatius and his soldiers were left to defend the castle at Pamplona without any support.

Many Navarrese citizens backed the French and attacked Ignatius and his men at the castle. Ignatius and his soldiers fought bravely but were eventually defeated. During the attack, Ignatius was severely injured. His leg was shattered when it was hit with a cannonball. Even though he was on the side of Spain, the Franco-Navarrese soldiers admired Ignatius for his courage and brought him back to his home in Loyola.

Since he could no longer fight, Ignatius went on to found the Society of Jesus, whose followers are known as Jesuits, and later was made a Catholic saint. Francis Xavier was also beatified for his efforts in founding the Jesuits. He was also a Basque who hailed from Navarre.

Battle of Esquíroz (Noáin)

In June 1521, French General André de Foix saw an opportunity to seize control of Navarre because Castile was involved in an uprising by the citizens. John III's son, Henry II, then called upon the French and Navarre to take on the Spanish forces. He mustered a force of about 10,000 men. The Spanish called for volunteers, and their newly formed troops numbered 30,000! At Esquíroz, which is near Pamplona, the French forces were defeated, and General André de Foix was captured.

Fall of Amaiur

After having an insufficient number of forces in the Battle of Esquíroz, the Franco-Navarrese mustered as many as 27,000 soldiers in their expedition to regain control of Navarre and the Basque areas. Many were French forces, and the others were Gascons (Basques). They marched toward the Bidasoa River in northern Navarre and then on to Baztan, where they placed a Castilian stronghold under siege. The Castilians then surrendered in exchange for unobstructed passage back to Castile.

Under the command of Guillaume Gouffier, the combined Franco-Navarrese troops captured the fortress of Urantzu and then moved upon Hondarribia in Gipuzkoa, a Basque province along the Bidasoa River. They captured the coastal fortification there.

In 1522, Holy Roman Emperor Charles V and his Castilian-Aragon forces left Pamplona with 7,000 men and marched to the fortress of Amaiur. The Navarrese forces consisted of only 200 knights, as they were awaiting reinforcements. The relief forces never arrived, and the fort fell rapidly. The Navarrese commanders were imprisoned in Pamplona, and two were deliberately poisoned.

In 1524, the Franco-Navarrese forces were promised restitution of their properties if they vowed allegiance to Emperor Charles V, which they did. Their properties, however, weren't fully restored, which led to sporadic clashes, mostly in Lower Navarre.

Fear of Witches

The Catholic Church and the Roman papacy had a great deal of political power in Europe. Charles V, the Holy Roman Emperor, spent many years dealing with the Muslims in the Ottoman Empire and with political alliances made between the Muslims and even the Christian kings, like Francis I of France. Charles V defended the Catholic Church from the pressures of Islam and the Protestant religions during his reign. Deviations from the teachings of the Bible, as interpreted by ordained priests, were viewed as contaminations of sacred scripture, and these people were often found guilty of heresy.

King Charlemagne (r. 800–814), who had imposed Catholicism upon France, stated, "If anyone, deceived by the devil, shall believe as is customary among pagans, that any man or woman is a night-witch, and eats men, and on that account burn that person to death and he shall be executed."

In Spain, Muslims controlled many territories. In the 16th century, Spain ordered all Muslims to convert to Catholicism, although they didn't do so until a century later. Also, during the 16th century, the Protestant Reformation started in Germany, where it soon spread throughout Europe. Heresy and witchcraft were often packaged together, and people sometimes believed that Protestants believed in supernatural beings. The rationale for connecting Protestantism with witchcraft was flawed.

The Ecclesiastical Inquisition

An inquisition was a tribunal established by the papacy to prevent misguided teachings and practices from infiltrating the population. That sometimes occurred when people had converted from another religious belief to Catholicism. Such tribunals were established in the 13th century and were reaffirmed in later centuries. Initially, the Dominican order was assigned the task of holding these ecclesiastical trials, but that was later transferred to the Jesuits.

The Basque Witch Trials

In 1525, in Navarre, a special commission was established to explore the mountainous regions of Navarre where the Basques lived. They had heard rumors that people had seen the "devil's mark" on women. The devil's mark was the appearance of a red or blue mark on the body made from the claw of a demon. Investigators were dispatched and returned with about thirty individuals.

Judge Pedro de Balanza, a royal magistrate, was sent out to "inquire, learn, correct, punish, and sentence the diabolical sect and the crimes committed by these witches who are said to be in this Kingdom of Navarra." Two girls, aged nine and eleven, came forward claiming to be "witch-finders." The number of people convicted is unknown, but judgment was said to have been swift, resulting in executions. Modern estimates believe about fifty were executed.

In 1534, an odd woman by the name of Maria Sagardoy was accused on the basis that she kept a dead toad on her porch. Her story was embroidered to the point that it was reported that she made concoctions and potions from parts of dead toads. Rumors spread that she poisoned people. She managed to escape prosecution because she said she was pregnant.

In 1540, another cluster of trials was conducted in the Salazar Valley in the Pyrenees. The accused were purportedly supposed to have "reneged God and with filth and burnt toads and other poisons, they have used poisoned powders to kill." According to Balanza, their followers "have gathered many times, both day and night, in their gatherings and festivities and dances of the witches." Their acts were called "maleficia."

In 1560, Graciana Belca was accused of using herbal mixtures to control others. She was an elderly woman, but she was still tortured on the rack and given water tortures. She was sentenced to one hundred lashings and then exiled for ten years. Because she suffered broken arms and was maimed, it is doubtful she survived. However, there is no record of what happened to her.

In 1575, Abbot Pedro de Anocibar, who wasn't an official magistrate, reported to the Royal Commission that Maria Johan had taken two young boys to a witches' gathering. Johan indicated to the abbot that she had been troubled by evil spirits most of her life, but she herself wasn't a witch. Two other Basque villagers were also accused, including a man and a woman. Poor Maria was burned at the stake in Pamplona. One of her assistants did too, but the other escaped. Hysteria took root, and in the course of seven months, seventeen more trials were held. All of the sentences aren't known, but many were accused of manipulating toads, attending covens, and poisoning crops. Most of these people were exiled.

The stories became even more preposterous. It was reported that women in white were seen floating above a house but then changed into cats, dogs, or pigs.

In 1609, Pierre de Lancre, a French judge, held the opinion that the Basque people, in particular, had a predilection for witchcraft. Sentences were more severe on the French side of the Basque Country. Pierre de Lancre was called upon as an inquisitor to resolve a dispute between some people with the lord of Urtubi. Urtubi is a town in the Basque province of Labourd. The citizens accused the lord and his followers of being witches. It was said that Urtubi's followers would "dance indecently, ate excessively; make love diabolically; perform acts of atrocious sodomy; blaspheme scandalously." They would also keep toads, lizards, and vipers, and it was said they engaged in passionate love-making with goats.

Pierre de Lancre's witch hunt in Labourd resulted in the executions of seventy Basques. De Lancre wanted to continue, but he was dismissed from office.

According to Basque mythology, their chief goddess, Mari, had helpers called *sorginaks*. A *sorginak* became equated with a demon who assists the devil or his legions. Because of that, the Basques became a target for those who were inundated with the mass hysteria that swept through Europe.

In Spain, Alonso de Salazar Frías, a priest and a lawyer, was selected as an inquisitor for the tribunal of Logroño (La Rioja) in 1609. Accusations streamed in, and by 1610, around six people were burned at the stake.

Salazar toured the region, collecting more evidence. He pledged to pardon anyone who "confessed." When he returned, he claimed to have information on as many as 1,800 individuals. Most of those people retracted their statements later.

Jurisdictional and Moral Issues

There were issues surrounding the jurisdiction for the courts in which witchcraft cases were held. In Madrid, there was the Inquisition Tribunal, and in Navarre, there was the Royal Council. For years, there were disputes over which court had the right to hear and decide these cases. The Royal Council of Navarre argued that since inquisitors didn't have to be lawyers, it had the right to try cases. Navarrese courts further argued that the Inquisitional courts only imposed penalties like confession and penance. The Royal Council, however, was empowered to deal with the secular aspects of these crimes, like the destruction of property or bodily harm. Witnesses gave conflicting accounts of supernatural occurrences. Others brought up incidents related to crop damage. On a subjective level, accusers could use the court to rid themselves of bad neighbors or people inflicted with mental illness.

These trials usually focused upon whether or not people were *malas Christians* (bad Christians) or *buena Christians* (good Christians), as defined by the Catholic Church. Cases were also influenced by the beliefs of local villagers and the personalities of those accused.

In later medieval courts, torture was considered a legitimate way of securing the "truth." To lend validity to a sentence, it was believed that testimonies by two "unimpeachable" individuals were invaluable. That way, convictions could be obtained despite a paucity of circumstantial evidence.

In many cases, the Royal Council of Navarre transferred cases to the Spanish Inquisition Tribunal. Their Sentences were usually lighter, and there were restrictions about physical torture. Executions couldn't be ordered without approval from the king. So, when judges felt a person shouldn't be dealt with severely, the accused were sent to Spain. However, there was a problem with that. Sometimes, the Inquisitional courts would impose a sentence of imprisonment, but conditions were so bad in the prisons that people died, particularly the elderly.

Autonomy/Home Rule in the Southern Basque Country

In 1451, Labourd was made a French autonomous province. In 1589, Lower Navarre was incorporated into France with the accession of King Henry IV.

The Southern Basque Country refers to those provinces that lie geographically within Spain: Biscay, Gipuzkoa, Álava, and Upper Navarre. Throughout the 13th and 14th centuries, the Basques had their own government consisting of oral traditions and common law. They had general councils called foral parliaments, each of which covered a province. These parliaments had elected representatives from among the local inhabitants.

During the Middle Ages, the provinces were divided into Basques *señoríos* or *jaurerriak* ("Basque lordships"). They were hereditary land titles to territories that were run by a count or a lord. The kings of various Basque areas, like the king of Pamplona, had to swear allegiance to that leader.

The *Fueros* in Spain

The charters, or *fueros*, of the individual Basque districts gave the Basques a degree of fiscal independence, a court system, control of the military draft, and constitutional rights of non-Castilian provinces. Castilian kings had to swear to observe Basque laws.

Difficulties arose when there were conflicts between laws in the local territories and the central government. For example, a person might be able to escape conviction by fleeing from Aragon to a Basque autonomous province.

In 1719, when the more absolutist Spanish monarch Philip V attempted to centralize his power, the Basque provinces were able to maintain their autonomy because they supported Philip in the War of Spanish Succession.

End of Home Rule in France

The historic Basque provinces of Labourd, Soule, and Lower Navarre were geographically located in France. In 1733 and in 1748, the Estates-General—the governing body in France—suppressed self-government in the Basque provinces for the purposes of taxation and control of the central government.

Labourd had been weakened by an economic downturn. A Basque patriot from Labourd, Dominique-Joseph Garat, vigorously defended Labourd's democratic status. By 1790, the Estates-General morphed into the National Assembly, and it abolished home rule in the Basque Country. In 1791, a new constitution was passed in France, confirming that.

War of the Pyrenees

The formidable Pyrenees
The original uploader was Nhamblen at Kiingereza Wikipedia., CC BY-SA 3.0 <http://creativecommons.org/licenses/by-sa/3.0/>, via Wikimedia Commons https://commons.wikimedia.org/wiki/File:Central_pyrenees.jpg

Between 1793 and 1795, the War of the Pyrenees was fought between the Kingdom of France and the Kingdoms of Spain and Portugal. The War of the Pyrenees was one of the many French Revolutionary Wars. Initially, Spain remained neutral, but when France declared war on Spain, they entered the war. The French army then recruited Basques from the French Basque provinces; this was a practice that continued into the 19th century. The French army invaded the province of Labourd, and there were many deaths (1,600 in all) and mass deportations. Many of the affected people fled to America.

To make the chronology easier to follow, the two theaters of this war have been split into separate sections.

War in the Eastern Pyrenees

In April of 1793, Spanish Captain General Antonio Ricardos commanded the Catalonian army. He invaded the region of Cerdagne and captured the commune of Saint-Laurent-de-Cerdans. Following that, he boldly defeated the poorly trained French troops at the Tech River, located right on the Spanish-French border in the county of Roussillon. The French were commanded by an elderly commander, Mathieu Henri Marchant de La Houlière, who became so depressed by his failure to defend the area that he committed suicide. Spain then divided their army into two divisions: the Army of the Eastern Pyrenees and the Army of the Western Pyrenees.

In May, Ricardos attacked a French encampment under the command of Louis-Charles de Flers near Mas Deu. Once the French were gone from there, Ricardos struck Fort de Bellegarde at the town of Le Perthus. He promptly placed it under siege. About a month and a half later, the French gave up the fort.

It was now July. Ricardos pursued the French toward Perpignan, the capital city of Roussillon. Ricardos separated his army into five columns. In the beginning, they made good progress. The third column even captured some hills there. However, the second column, under Jerónimo Girón-Moctezuma, Marquis de las Amarillas, was delayed and failed to support the third column like he was supposed to. Louis-Charles de Flers then attacked the separated third column and forced it back. Another column turned around to help, and they were able to reform their position. But then the French attacked full-force. Unfortunately, the columns were too far apart, and the French defeated them.

During the following months, the war went both ways. At times, the French were able to repel the Spanish back, and at others, the Spanish were able to win some solid victories.

In December 1793, the Portuguese allied with Ricardos. This combined force won a victory in the Battle of Villelongue-dels-Monts. This was followed by the Battle of Collioure at the end of the month, which saw the Spanish winning the French ports of Collioure and Port-Vendres.

Ricardos went to Madrid to ask for reinforcements. The weather up in the mountains was cold and wet, and it took its toll on Ricardos, who was sixty-six years old. Ricardos died of pneumonia in March. His successor, Alejandro O'Reilly, died ten days later. Luis Firmin de Carvajal was then given command of the Army of Catalonia. The French also took on a new commander, Jacques François Dugommier.

In April of 1794, Dugommier returned to Boulou to expel the Spanish. He was successful, as he managed to force the Spanish to abandon their equipment. In May, the French recaptured the port of Collioure and took 7,000 Spanish from the garrison there as prisoners.

Dugommier then placed a siege upon the Spanish-held fort in Bellegarde. In August, the Spanish attempted to relieve the siege, but it was unsuccessful, and the starving soldiers were forced to surrender. Many had already starved to death.

In November of 1794, the Spanish troops were joined by the Portuguese. The French defeated them at the Battle of the Black Mountain. It was a tough battle for both sides. Dugommier died early in the battle and was replaced by Dominique Catherine de Pérignon. Luis de Carvajal, who led the Spanish, also died. The Spanish/Portuguese suffered extreme losses, as estimates believe that 10,000 were killed or wounded, and 8,000 were captured. The French lost less, although it was still a great number; it is believed 3,000 were killed or wounded.

War in the Western Pyrenees

In February of 1794, the French under Commanders Jean Henri Guy Nicholas de Frégeville and Augustin Lespinasse were able to hold their hilltop positions and fortress during the Battle of Sans Culottes Camp against the Spanish cavalry and infantry under José Urrutia y de las Casas. Losses on both sides were small.

In March, the Spanish Basques were assigned to guard the borders of Sara, Itxassou, and Ascain against any incoming French troops. They didn't and instead fled back to the Basque Country. As a punishment, the residents of the Basque villages were herded into carts and taken to the Landes, a large wooded area in Gascony. Their valuables were taken, and it is believed that thousands were taken from their homes, with around 1,600 dying in the process.

In July, the French Army of the Western Pyrenees attacked the Spanish positions, which led to the Battle of the Baztan Valley. The commander of the French army, Bon-Adrien Jeannot de Moncey, led his forces to a decisive victory over the Spanish. The French proceeded along the Bidasoa River and snatched the town of Hondarribia.

The following month, the city of San Sebastián in Gipuzkoa surrendered to the French. The nobles of San Sebastián attempted to negotiate with the French. They claimed they supported the French revolutionary ideals and made a petition to be joined to France. However, they had caveats to that proposal; they wanted French respect for their regional laws, the freedom to practice Catholicism, and a set of rules for the management of war-related issues. The French refused to accept the conditions, and the Gipuzkoa representatives were imprisoned or exiled. When General Moncey heard this, he came out in support of the governmental institutions of Gipuzkoa, which enraged the authorities in

Madrid. As a result, the Spanish lashed out at the Basque residents living in Gipuzkoa. When the representatives were released from their imprisonment (those that survived at least), they were accused of high treason by Spanish authorities and placed on trial.

In October, Moncey moved into Navarre, and the French proved victorious in the Battle of Orbaitzeta. The Spanish then gave up their territory north of Pamplona, and they also lost their arms foundry at Eugi and Orbaitzeta.

Winter was setting in, and Moncey headed home. The winter was harsh, and Moncey lost many men to disease and the cold. The following year, the French came back in full force. In July 1795, both Vitoria and Bilbao fell to the French, ending the war and leading to the Peace of Basel.

The Peace of Basel

Manuel Godoy, First Secretary of State of Spain, was concerned that the province of Gipuzkoa would try to cede to France, as they had wished to do at the beginning of the war. In exchange for Gipuzkoa, Godoy gave up two-thirds of the Caribbean island of Hispaniola to France. Upon the request of French commander Moncey, amendments were added to the agreement, stating that Spain would make no reprisals against those Basques who had expressed allegiance to France. This treaty was signed in 1795.

The Ineffective Bayonne Statute

In 1804, Napoleon Bonaparte crowned himself emperor of France. In 1808, Napoleon invaded and conquered Spain. He named his brother, Joseph, as the new king of Spain. The Bayonne Statute was negotiated with Joseph Bonaparte. This statute specifically had wording in it that recognized the Basque principality, allowing for a degree of home rule. This statute was virtually ignored in practice.

In 1812, the Spanish Constitution, also known as the Constitution of Cádiz, was passed. However, the Constitution of Cádiz totally overlooked the Basque Country altogether. It specified that Spain was a nation in its own right. Because no allowances were made recognizing the *fueros*—the charters—of the Basque districts, the Basque population was concerned they would lose any chance of having a self-government. As a result, deputies were sent to Cádiz in order to clear this up. They called upon the Parliament of Navarre to make this change. However, their plea was turned down.

At the heart of the Basque issue was the overlapping Peninsular War, which was fought between Britain, Portugal, and France over the leadership of Spain. In 1814, after that war, Joseph Bonaparte abdicated the throne of Spain, and power was restored to the former monarch, Ferdinand VII. King Ferdinand was an absolute monarch. With the ascendancy of Ferdinand, a return to orthodoxy took place. Catholicism was the mandatory religion in Spain and in the Basque Country.

The three provinces where the Basque regions lay in France—Labourd, Soule, and Lower Navarre—were under French jurisdiction. The Basques who lived there were recruited into the armed forces of France. This area is what is called the French Basque Country today.

Chapter 7 – The Modern Period

The First Carlist War in Spain, 1833–1840

In 1833, Queen Isabella II took the throne, but she wasn't even three years old. Don Carlos María Isidro Benito de Borbón was the younger son of Charles IV and became a pretender to the throne under the name of Charles V. He was more traditional and supported the cause of Basque autonomy.

The Basque supporters of Don Carlos rallied under the military leadership of Basque Tomás de Zumalacárregui, and an army was formed, which was financed by the Basque provinces in Spain. Carlism, named after Don Carlos, which was essentially a Spanish political movement, supported Don Carlos as the legitimate heir to the Spanish throne as opposed to Isabella II. It eventually morphed into an ideological conflict between conservatives and liberals in the Basque provinces. The Basques became alarmed, as they thought they would never regain home rule they had once achieved through the *fueros*, which had been abolished by the former Spanish Constitution.

The Spanish Basques decided to join the army that represented the traditionalists. They were concerned that a more liberal stance would further threaten their rights to rule themselves, as it wouldn't help their cause for maintaining some level of self-government.

The Basque Motivations

The Basques were highly skilled masters of the sea in the areas of northern Spain and southwestern France. The Basques had numerous ports and established trade routes, and the late King Ferdinand VII of Spain had been pleased with that arrangement. However, the Constitution of Cádiz eliminated home rule and the *fueros*. The Basques were promised that Charles, the contender to the throne, would protect their individual freedoms and reestablish the *fueros*. However, this war pitted Basque against Basque, as not all the Basques believed in Don Carlos, although the vast majority did.

In 1834, Zumalacárregui and the Basques descended from the mountains into Álava and defeated General Manuel O'Doyle. By 1835, nearly all of Gipuzkoa and Biscay were in Carlist hands.

Zumalacárregui eventually started to rely upon supplies confiscated from the enemy and was forced into fighting a guerilla war. The Carlists wanted to gain control of the seaports, but Zumalacárregui preferred to march to Madrid and claim the throne for Don Carlos. Zumalacárregui obeyed his orders, though, and besieged Bilbao in 1835. He was wounded there, and due to some poor medical attention, he died. Subsequent clashes turned against the Carlists. Some of the contemporary supporters of Basque governance, like John Francis Bacon, didn't trust Carlos to keep his agreement to establish home rule, saying that Carlos "would quickly find excuses for infringing them."

In 1839, the Convention of Vergara, also known as the "Embrace of Vergara," ended the First Carlist War. By virtue of that treaty, Basque home rule was modified, along with the *fueros*. A follow-up act, the Compromise Act of 1841, dissolved the Kingdom of Navarre, making it a Spanish province. However, Navarre retained its control over taxation within its province.

Economic Consequences

After the First Carlist War, General Espartero became the regent for young Isabella II. As a result of the war, the treasury was depleted. Trade, which had greatly benefited Pamplona, fell dramatically because the trade between Pamplona and Bayonne had all but ceased once the customs were moved by the French government in the French Basque provinces. Also, some common lands were confiscated by the French government, leaving many French Basques poverty-stricken. Famines occurred, and there was a massive emigration to the United States by the French Basques.

The Third Carlist War, 1872–1876

Although there was a Second Carlist War in Spain, it didn't affect the Basques that much. The Third Carlist War, however, was crucial for the Basque Country. The Spanish government was unstable, having gone through a high turnover of government officials, and the poor economic situation in the country contributed to the discontent of the Spanish people. Back in 1868, Queen Isabella II abdicated the throne and was succeeded by an Italian prince, Amadeo I, rather than a Spaniard, which gave rise to popular resentment.

The Carlists supported Carlos VII, the new pretender to the throne, and recruited the Basques to rise up against the Spanish government in 1872. The Basques established a temporary state of their own in the Spanish provinces of Álava, Biscay, Gipuzkoa, and Navarre. They demanded the restoration of home rule and charters, like the *fueros* of the past. The Basques also wanted an exemption from the Spanish military draft, as they did not wish to fight in their wars.

Despite the fact they weren't well-equipped, the Basques occupied some Spanish towns, including Estella and La Seu d'Urgell in Navarre, and laid siege to the cities of San Sebastián and Bilbao. The Carlists then set up the town of Estella as their new temporary capital.

The First Spanish Republic, 1873–1874

Unfortunately, the Basques weren't successful with their sieges of San Sebastián or Bilbao, but they did gain the attention of both France and Spain to their cause. In 1873, Amadeo I abdicated, and Spain set up the First Spanish Republic until they could resolve the succession crisis. In December of the following year, Alfonso XII, the son of Queen Isabella II, was made the king of Spain.

Although the monarchy was reestablished, the Carlists continued fighting. Many Carlists either flocked to the other side or were put on trial, so the remaining Carlists mostly tried to hold on to the positions they had after this point. The Carlist general Torcuato Mendiri was able to score a victory at Lácar, and he was also able to capture military equipment from the government troops and take hundreds of prisoners. About a thousand men died in this battle, mostly those from the government forces. Sadly, Mendiri wasn't able to repeat his victory in 1875, and he was forced to retreat from the government forces. Following that, he was dismissed. His replacement, Prince Alfonso, Count of Caserta, wasn't able to stop the government's advance, despite the fact he had a lot of equipment and men at his disposal.

By 1876, the Carlists were losing ground and had to surrender the town of Estella. Once Estella was lost, the Carlists lost heart and fled. Even Carlos VII, the pretender, left Spain altogether. In February of 1876, King Alfonso XII marched into the Basque city of Pamplona in triumph.

After the Third Carlist War, the Basque provinces lost their home rule and were placed under martial law. The Spanish government then entered into negotiations with the Basques for what came to be called the Basque Economic Agreement.

Basque Economic Agreement

Because of the unique needs of the Basque people, an economic agreement was reached with Spain in 1878 related to taxation. This agreement stated that the Basque provinces were "to pay taxes according to their means, in the same way as other Spaniards." However, the Spanish government did present a certain quota they expected based on past performance. The *fueros* of the past were abolished, but provincial councils were allowed to continue as before, which would develop their own system for the collection of taxes.

Besides the taxes placed on individuals, there were set taxes, such as territorial taxes (property), industrial taxes (for example, on the production of iron), taxes on the transfer of money, a stamp tax, and a consumption tax.

Rise of Basque Nationalism in the 19th Century

The Basques in France became politically polarized between the Royalists and the Republicans. Most of the Basques were Royalists, which was a party that was identified with Catholicism. After the War of the Pyrenees, French was considered the national language. As time went on, the Basques began to speak their own language in the Basque communities.

The Basques in France became more involved in the economy when the railway through Aquitaine was completed in 1864. The mingling of Basque and non-Basque peoples took place, and tourism even arrived.

Even though the Basques in the Spanish areas fared somewhat better than the French after the Carlist Wars, the Spanish never really appreciated the uniqueness of the Basque cultures or practices as they once had when the *fueros* were in place. Although no one could really annihilate the use of the Basque language, especially in the Basque provinces, they tried.

In the Spanish Parliament, Sabino Arana created the Basque Nationalist Party in 1895. Initially, the Basque Nationalists were somewhat xenophobic. De Arana was a purist and believed that the Basque race was morally superior and likewise supported anti-liberal Catholicism. He believed all members should be able to prove Basque ancestry. He discouraged the immigration of non-Basque Spaniards and strongly encouraged Basques to marry only within the Basque community and to speak the Basque language.

Chapter 8 – Economy

Expert Seaman

The Basques have been and still are excellent seamen, fishermen, and shipbuilders. The well-known French explorer Samuel de Champlain once said the Basques were "the cleverest men at this fishing." He was specifically referring to their whaling skills.

The Basques had a wide coastline that opened out to the Bay of Biscay and used their ports on the northern coast to sail tow Ireland and northern England, where they conducted a hefty trade. Whale oil was used in lamps in the early days; whale blubber could be used to manufacture soap, cosmetics, and in the manufacturing of leather.

Local Whaling

Whaling in the 18th century; it was treacherous but lucrative.
https://en.wikipedia.org/wiki/File:FMIB_39769_Northern_Whale_Fishery_(Zorgdrager,_1720).jpeg

Whaling was more common among the Basques in Spain, especially in the ports of Gipuzkoa and the Biscay provinces, than in France. King Sancho VI, also known as Sancho the Wise, who served as the king of Navarre in the 12th century, had created a successful whaling industry for the Basques. Whaling fared quite well until the end of the 19th century. Sancho VI granted certain privileges to the town of San Sebastián, allowing the people there to distribute and house whaling products. He also had his seamen concentrate on the city of Bayonne, where they had a brisk market. Duties had to be paid on the storage of these products, which increased cash flow.

Of course, whaling is discouraged today, but at that time, there were sufficient whales in the area, so it had no significant impact until later centuries when overexploitation diminished the whale population off the Bay of Biscay and in the North Atlantic fishing areas.

North Atlantic Fishing

Whaling accelerated off the coast of England and continued to be lucrative through the years. This was beneficial for both the Basques and the English, who, in turn, prepared the whale products and shipped them overseas, sending them as far as Brazil. In Brazil, Basque whalers instructed the Brazilians in the trade and in the development of new uses for whale blubber (for instance, whale blubber could be used as lubrication for their machinery in the sugar mills). The Brazil trade came to a screeching halt when some Basque sailors cut down trees for brazilwood. Brazilwood is extremely useful in making masts for ships. Portugal, which controlled the colony of Brazil, was incensed, as they had a royal monopoly on the product.

Through the years, the Basque whaling industry ran head-first into difficulties with foreign interests, such as Iceland and northern Norway. Those countries resented infringement by Basque whalers, as whaling was a part of their history as well. The Basques were able to conduct business for a while, but they eventually had to abandon those waters after foreigners destroyed some of their gear in retribution for the incursions. Piracy and plundering sometimes took place at sea when English ships attacked them. Even Danish ships seized barrels of blubber when the Basques came into port to sell them. Human interference started to become even more dangerous than the actual process of whaling.

Industrial Expansion

The Basques lost a lot of advantages after the suppression of the *fueros* following the Carlist Wars. The Biscay area used to produce high-quality iron, which they sold locally, but in the 19th century, they began exporting the ore to Great Britain, which was more profitable. The entrepreneurial Basques reinvested it in developing equipment and machinery to develop more advanced iron and steel products for export. This touched off a "mini-industrial boom."

To keep up with demand, foreigners were hired. Most spoke Spanish, but they had different cultures than the Basques. In addition, these newcomers weren't investors. They were very poor and looking for any steady job they could find.

The railway system that had recently been put in place was excellent for shipping products to other areas of the Basque Country and to ports for overseas shipping. The railroad also helped develop the coastal areas, where resorts were built for tourists. Since the Basques had many buildings there with Romanesque architecture, sightseeing often occurred.

Mining

In the 19th century, Biscay's industries expanded exponentially. One of the earliest iron factories was called Santa Ana de Bolueta. The population of the area nearly doubled, as the Basque people migrated there for work. Another city named Barakaldo grew quickly as well. This city had a dynamite factory to service the mines, and that, in turn, triggered the erection of a steelwork plant. The Basques hired other Basques from the inland areas, but there weren't enough workers, as the Basques had lost so many of their people to emigration. As a result, they had to depend upon immigrant labor. By the latter part of the 19th century, the humble province of Biscay was the world's leading exporter of iron ore.

The quality of their ore was quite high, and during that era, foreign investors took a keen interest in the Basque iron mines. Britain was its largest client. In 1902, Altos Hornos de Vizcaya was established. It was the merger of three businesses: Altos Hornos de Bilbao, La Vizcaya, and La Iberia. Over ninety million tons of ore were extracted at its peak level of production.

Most of the mines were in the hands of the Basque elite and wealthy. In fact, just a small number of clan families—namely, the Chavarri and Ibarra—owned half of the mining interests. Their mines produced over 60 percent of the iron in Spain. Unfortunately, this forced smaller companies to go out of business.

The Basques needed the coal produced in the province of Asturias to the west to fuel their iron industry, but the Asturians had to depend upon unreliable and expensive rail services to transport it to Biscay. So, the Basques had to get coal from the British, who sold it cheaper. Thus, foreigners didn't invest in the coal mines, as they made less profit from them. Spain also charged very high tariffs for its exports, which caused a decline in orders. It was only during the First World War that the Basques and the Asturians were able to turn a profit. After the war, however, the coal and iron industries went into a crisis.

In Gipuzkoa province, the textile industries flourished. There were textile companies such as Algodonera de San Antonio and paper factories in Oria and Tolosa. By 1920, there were more fabric companies and a small sewing machine company, which was simply called Alfa.

Chapter 9 – The Twentieth Century

Basque Nationalism

After the Carlist Wars of the 19th century, there was an emigration of Basques to the Americas. To keep up with demands for trade, foreigners came into the Basque Country. However, the Basques desperately wanted to preserve their unique culture and language, and the Basques felt that these immigrants were threatening the integrity of their culture and language. In 1931, the Basque Nationalist Party and the Republicans worked together to develop the Statute of Estella, which called for the creation of an autonomous state for the Spanish Basque counties of Álava, Biscay, and Gipuzkoa. It didn't receive enough support because of divisions among the Carlists. A more abridged version was proposed, but political events interceded, thus delaying any action.

The Second Spanish Republic, 1931–1939

The initiation of the Second Spanish Republic in 1931 brought about an ambivalent reaction from the Basques. The provinces of Biscay, Gipuzkoa, and, to a limited extent, Álava supported the Republicans. Even though the leftist Republicans maintained an anti-Catholic policy, they did support a degree of autonomy for the Basques. Navarre, though, was opposed to the new republic. They had legal difficulties regarding the validity of the voting process and arguments about the nomenclature used to identify it.

The Short-Lived Statute of Autonomy of the Basque Country of 1936

In 1936, the leading political faction, the Republicans, achieved the long-desired passage of the Statute of Autonomy of the Basque Country. It protected the traditional privileges granted to the Basques from the past. José Antonio Aguirre took over leadership of the state of "Euskadi," becoming the first president of the Basque Country. His first act was to muster forces to go up against the rival faction in the ongoing Spanish Civil War. Aguirre formed a conciliatory government composed of socialists, communists, Republicans, and Nationalists.

The Spanish Civil War, 1936–1939

This war pitted a myriad of organizations fighting for the control of Spain and the kind of government Spain would embrace. One side, generally called the Republicans, represented groups that even espoused conflicting ideologies. Despite their differences, they adamantly opposed the other side, called the Nationalists. The Basques were aligned with the Republicans.

Manuel Azaña was the leader of the Republicans. This side also had the support of the regular Spanish army, called Ejército Popular de la República ("People's Army of the Republic). There were many other groups as well, each with its own agenda:

The Popular Front - included socialists, communists, Valencian nationalists, and others. The Valencian nationalists supported a separate national state for the people of the Catalonia region.

The UGT (Unión General de Trabajadores, or General Union of Workers) - a Spanish labor union.

The CNT-FAI (Confederación Nacional del Trabajo, or National Confederation of Labour/Federación Anarquista Ibérica, or Iberian Anarchist Federation) -anarchist organizations that were closely linked.

The Generalitat de Catalunya, or Government of Catalonia - the self-government of Catalonia in northeastern Spain.

Euzko Gudarostea - the Basque army.

International Brigades - military units supported by the communists.

The Nationalists were led by General Francisco Franco. Franco sought to return Spain back into the embrace of the monarchy, preferably with him as the leader.

Francisco Franco
Unknown authorUnknown author, CC0, via Wikimedia Common
https://commons.wikimedia.org/wiki/File:RETRATO_DEL_GRAL._FRANCISCO_FRANCO_B AHAMONDE_(adjusted_levels).jpg

The Nationalist groups are listed below:

The FET y de las JONS (Falange Española Tradicionalista y de las Juntas de Ofensiva Nacional Sindicalista, or Traditionalist Spanish Phalanx and that of the Councils of the National Syndicalist Offensive) – a party that supported the former Carlists and the candidacy of Francisco Franco.

The FE de las JONS (Falange Española de las Juntas de Ofensiva Nacional Sindicalista, or Spanish Phalanx of the National Syndicalist Offensive) – the Fascists; in 1936, it combined with the FET y de las JONS to become the only legal party of Spain.

The Requetés – a group that supported a splinter faction of the former Carlists.

The Renovación Española, or Spanish Renovation – Royalists who supported the restoration of the former monarch.

The Army of Africa – specifically Morocco, which was a Spanish colony at the time.

Italy – Italy, which was ruled by Fascists, supported Franco.

Germany – Germany, led by Adolf Hitler, supported Franco and his Nationalist Party to create support for himself and his future plans.

Francisco Franco of the Nationalists had his sights on capturing Madrid and destroying the Second Spanish Republic. However, before moving to Madrid, he decided to attempt to gain possession of the province of Biscay, along with all of its ports along the Bay of Biscay.

The Bombing of Guernica

Franco was very much opposed to the Basques and what they stood for. On April 26th, 1937, his German supporters sent out the Luftwaffe's Condor Legion—the Nazi German air force that assisted in the Spanish Civil War—which heavily bombed the town of Guernica in Biscay. There were five waves of bombings, and the aircraft carried between 100 and 110 pounds of bombs. Three-quarters of the town was destroyed. Roads leading in and out of the city center were blown apart. Oddly enough, the arms factory wasn't destroyed, nor was the Gernikako Arbola ("The Tree of Gernika"), the oak tree that symbolized the Basque civilization. There are varying estimates of the death toll from this attack. Eyewitnesses at the time believe there were about 1,700 casualties.

Tree of Gernika

Battle of Bilbao

Aguirre's government only held power until June of 1937, which was when the Nationalists attacked Bilbao. An "iron ring" was built to protect the government. This was a ring of hastily constructed fortifications around the capital city. The ring was easily breached during the Battle of

Bilbao. With the fall of Bilbao, Aguirre and the government moved to Trucios, Catalonia, and Santander successively. The Republican army went to Santander to negotiate a deal, but Franco canceled any agreement and imprisoned 22,000 of them. Some were freed, but others remained in prison. Five hundred seventy men were executed.

In August to September of 1937, the campaign moved to the province of Aragon. The Republicans, under Commander Enrique Lister, had a huge infantry force backed up by tanks and aircraft. The Nationalists depended exclusively on infantry, but they had a huge number of men. This campaign was a Republican victory, but they failed to gain significant ground.

The Republicans still had a significant amount of territory in Cantabria, so they moved their offensive there. Unfortunately for the Republicans, the Nationalists had nearly doubled the number of forces.

The Republicans launched two attacks against the Nationalists, but both attempts failed, which led to the Basques losing control of Bilboa. The barbarity of this attack was memorialized by the famous painter Pablo Picasso in his work, Guernica.

The End before the End

With the help of the masterful Basque sailors, the Republicans secured control of a number of coastal cities. However, Franco's forces overran the Republican forces in mainland Spain, and it didn't help that Madrid was placed under siege in November of 1936. The Republicans were able to stave off the Nationalists for quite some time.

The "Santoña Treason"

After enduring that savage attack, the Basques surrendered, doing so before the Spanish Civil War was over. The Italian forces represented Franco, and they signed the Santoña Agreement, in which the Basque army would surrender. Following that, the captured Basque soldiers would be treated as prisoners of war according to international law.

When Franco saw the agreement, he trashed it and imprisoned 22,000 captured Basque soldiers. Three hundred were freed several months later, but 510 were executed. The rest remained in prison for an unspecified period of time. Hence, the Santoña Agreement was dubbed the "Santoña Treason."

In 1938, the Nationalists drove through the Republican forces, cutting them in two. Franco then turned to Catalonia and captured Barcelona, which was its capital. Seeing that they were losing, the Republicans offered to make a settlement. Franco refused their overture and kept on fighting.

Door-to-door fighting during the Spanish Civil War
https://commons.wikimedia.org/wiki/File:Nationalist_soldiers_raiding_Madrid,_March_1937.jpg

The Battle of Madrid

The Republicans knew they had the advantage when it came to Madrid, but Nationalist Emilio Mola wasn't going to let that stop him. On November 8th, 1936, he attacked Madrid. German Panzer I tanks came thundering in, while bombs from the German Condor Legion dropped from the sky. Republican forces fought back with their rifles and a rationed amount of ammunition. They knew they were outmatched, and some tried to flee, but Republican General José Miaja prevented them, saying they should die rather than run like cowards.

A modest relief force arrived to support the Nationalists, but they were poorly trained. Their lack of skill gave the Republicans a boost of confidence. On November 9th, a Republican force attacked the Nationalists at the Casa de Campo and forced them back.

On November 12th, a Republican force arrived to help. They attacked Cerro de los Ángeles Hill in order to prevent the Nationalists from cutting off routes to southern Spain. The confusion of languages confounded that effort, but luckily, the road to Valencia in southern Spain was accessible.

On November 19th, the Nationalists attacked the University City quarter in the heart of Madrid. Door-to-door fighting ensued. Counterattacks from the Republicans occurred throughout this district, as they were not willing to go without a fight. Franco realized he was losing a lot of his infantry due to the relentless attacks of the Republicans, and he made the hard decision of pulling them out so he could try and mitigate his losses.

Since the ground invasion did not work, Franco turned to aerial bombardment. It is hard to say if this invasion was worth it. The causalities were rather low, and people around the world condemned the action since it was one of the first bombings of civilians in history.

The fighting continued. At times, both sides would be so worn out that the fighting would briefly stop, but no one was taking a definitive lead. However, this changed in early 1939. By that point, only Madrid and a few other strongholds were left under Republican control. Madrid fell in late March, and Valencia, the last major holdout, surrendered soon after.

Francisco Franco entered Madrid and declared victory on April 1st, 1939.

<u>Atrocities</u>

There were mass atrocities committed during this war, as there were so many smaller factions who had their own ideological differences.

Within the first few months, 7,000 priests, monks, and nuns were executed by the Nationalists. Nationalist fighters raped Republican women. During 1940, 500,000 people were sent to concentration camps. Many of those were Spanish refugees hoping to find refuge in France, but as soon as they arrived, they were sent to concentration camps. The estimates of people executed after the war numbered 250,000.

The Republicans were also guilty of committing atrocities. Most notably, the Republicans targeted clergy and those civilians they believed to be Nationalist sympathizers. The number of how many people actually died is hard to estimate, as Franco's regime inflated the numbers for propaganda purposes, but it is believed to be around 50,000.

It is estimated that up to a million people were killed in the Spanish Civil War. It was the bloodiest and most brutal in Spanish history.

The French Basques during World War II

Just a year after the Spanish Civil War ended, the French Basque Country was occupied by the German military. The French government moved from Paris to Vichy, setting up in what was called the Free Zone. Areas within the small province of Soule and the eastern areas of Lower Navarre in France were within this zone. The Basques were supportive of the Vichy regime. Philippe Pétain was Chief of State of Vichy France.

Vichy France, although it was essentially a Nazi client state, conducted secret operations to resist the German occupation, which was, at the time, enmeshed in World War II. Northern France, including the French Basque Country, was under German control until the end of the war. Any Spanish Basques who may have fled Spain were immediately thrown into concentration camps.

Basque Code-Talkers

Because Euskara, the Basque language, was so different from the Indo-European languages, some Basques living in the United States, China, and the Philippines were used as "code-talkers." A code-talker is someone who speaks an uncommon language. These code-talkers helped the Allied war effort by transmitting secret messages to American troops operating in the Pacific theater. It was said that Lieutenants Nemesio Aguirre and Fernández Bakaicoa sent a couple of messages about the Battle of Guadalcanal. There was a desire to hire more Basque code-talkers, but there weren't enough of them living within a free country to recruit. So, Native Americans were mostly employed for that duty.

Francisco Franco

Francisco Franco became the president of Spain after the Spanish Civil War. He discussed the possibility of getting involved with Adolf Hitler and the Nazi regime in World War II, but the concessions he wanted didn't appeal to Hitler. Franco also realized his military limitations, especially if his navy had to go up against that of Great Britain. He was once thanked by Winston Churchill for not blocking entry to the Allies at Gibraltar: "In the dark days of the war the attitude of the Spanish government in not giving our enemies passage through Spain was extremely helpful to us." In reality, Franco knew he couldn't block the passage at Gibraltar militarily, nor resist the Allies from getting some occasional help from him, such as aiding American pilots who had to bail out over Spain. However, Franco did give some aid to Hitler. For example, he permitted the Spanish to voluntarily join the Axis forces if they so wished.

He executed his political foes or put them into labor camps under inhumane conditions. Historians estimate that between 30,000 to 50,000 died due to his oppression.

Franco's Campaign against the Basques

Franco outlawed the Basque Nationalists, calling them communists, and banned the use of the Basque language. Franco was a fervent anti-communist, and he attempted to associate the Basques with communists to give himself an excuse to imprison them. Resistance associations formed, which were created out of the Basque political parties: the EAJ-PNV (Basque National Party—the acronym stands for the Spanish and the French spelling of the party), the Basque Nationalist Action, the Basque division of the Spanish Socialist Party, and the Basque Republican Left. Whenever any of those groups tried to schedule an activity, Franco had them arrested. Because of his fondness for imprisonment and executions, the Basque Nationalists went underground.

In 1951, about 250,000 workers in Álava and Navarre went on strike. Franco responded swiftly with beatings, dismissals from their jobs, and imprisonments. The EAJ-PNV, though, undertook other activities, such as holding Basque music festivals, art shows, and the narration of old folktales related to their culture. In hiding, they taught Euskara, the Basque language, to their children.

There were terrorist attacks during Franco's term of office that were sponsored by the underground organization ETA, which stands for Euskadi Ta Askatasuna ("Basque Homeland and Liberty"). It was a far-left organization, and its stated goal was total independence for all the Basque provinces in both Spain and France. ETA members even assassinated a contender for the next presidency, Luis Carrero Blanco, who held the same political views as Franco. In addition, ETA carried out other violent terrorist attacks.

During his rule, Franco employed GAL, which were death squads, to put a halt to any forms of terrorism. He also assigned GAL the task of killing any people he considered threats to his administration. That included ETA.

The first ETA member to be killed in action was Txabi Etxebarrieta in 1968. He was killed by the Civil Guard (Spain's oldest law enforcement agency), and his funeral attracted many people. Etxebarrieta's death was compared to that of Jesus Christ, and it was said that he died for the sake of the "religion" of the oppressed motherland. A well-known Basque sculptor, Jorge Oteiza, designed a Pietá-type figure in the church where Etxebarrieta was buried. He is considered to be a Basque patriot today.

Transition to Democracy

Francisco Franco died in 1975, and Juan Carlos I became the king of Spain. Although Carlos told Franco he would continue his policies, he had no intention of doing so. He had witnessed the extreme repression of Franco and its sad aftermath. Although Franco had brought prosperity to the country, Carlos was saddened by the brutality of Franco's reign. There would, no doubt, be repercussions from that.

The Spanish Constitution of 1978 was passed, granting democratic reforms, including the suitable representation of the various provinces within the country. It was not a constitution in the strict sense, as observed by most other countries. It was deliberately open-ended. Spain is decentralized in the sense that it has different autonomous communities within its fifty provinces, each with its own specific laws. However, they had to answer to a higher power, which was the king and the overall administration of Spain.

According to Article 151 of the Spanish Constitution, the Statute of Autonomy of the Basque Country was passed in 1979. Each Basque community had its own constitution, which was voted upon by a three-quarters majority of each province. Each province had its own parliament, a legislative assembly, a council with an elected president and advisors (who were also elected by the assembly), and its own court of justice. They were allowed to levy and collect taxes, but the Basques had to contribute to the Spanish government for national defense, foreign affairs, maintenance of airports and public facilities for international commerce and travel, and ports.

This statute guaranteed liberties for the people of the provinces of Gipuzkoa, Álava, and Biscay. It put into place a parliamentary government with representatives elected by the Basque people. This statute also established universal suffrage and granted the Basques power to regulate industries, agriculture, tax collection, policing, and transportation. Euskara, the Basque language, was now permissible, along with Spanish.

Navarre chose to set up a chartered community, which is similar to an autonomous community. It controlled functions similar to that of the other three Basque provinces, although their political parties reflect a slight deviation, as there were pro-Basque parties and pro-Spanish parties. The pro-Basque parties heavily outnumber those of Spanish origin to this day. There is a movement inside Navarre to merge the province into the same autonomous status shared by the other three Basque provinces. Both the Basque language and Spanish is spoken in Navarre today.

Chapter 10 – Basque Terrorism

The Basque Nationalist Movement had to go underground during Franco's administration. During that time, they kept their movement alive and espoused total freedom for the Basque regions in Spain and France. At the heart of the Basque Nationalist Movement was the group ETA, whose name means "Basque Homeland and Liberty."

The introduction of democratic reforms and the Statute of Autonomy of the Basque Country appended to the Spanish Constitution fell short of ETA's goals for independence. From 1978 and onward, they staged a continual string of terrorist attacks.

There were thirteen fatal attacks during that period of time. For example, in May of 1978, a bomb exploded on a street in Pamplona, killing a Civil Guard in his passing vehicle. In September of 1978, two Civil Guards were killed by ETA gunmen; in May of 1980, three National Police officers were shot by ETA gunmen in the town of San Sebastián; in November of 1980, five people were killed, which included Civil Guards and a civilian; and in May of 1981, three Spanish military men were killed, and a bomb exploded in a Spanish destroyer. ETA was financed initially through robberies but later on through extortion.

ETA initiated a new group in the French Basque Country, the Iparretarrak ("the Northerners"). It was more of an anarchist group. Another group, the Comandos Autónomos Anticapitalistas ("Autonomous Anticapitalist Commandos"), also started carrying out terrorist attacks.

Failed Coup D'état

In 1981, when the country was in the process of electing Leopoldo Calvo-Sotelo as the new president, the Civil Guard and members of the army marched into the meeting room of the Congress of Deputies, with guns drawn. The coup failed, and Calvo-Sotelo was elected, but a three-way split in the political parties made it impossible for him to get sufficient support in the legislature. New elections were called for in 1982, and this time, Felipe González Márquez was elected.

Newly formed GAL were formed, even though they were illegal. These death squads murdered twenty-seven people. More were most likely killed, but those are the confirmed killings linked to them. Many injuries were also recorded as the result of bomb attacks. They targeted ETA members primarily and those of other leftist terrorist organizations. GAL performed these illegal executions from 1983 to 1987. This period was dubbed "Spain's dirty war." The people responsible for these killings were brought to court. Trials against them were initiated and continued for many years. To this day, people are still trying to discover what actually happened during "Spain's dirty war."

During that time, the Spanish government and ETA held negotiations, with occasional ceasefires being in effect. ETA members often hid on the French side of the border, where they trained and purchased arms. In 1987, France decided to no longer turn a blind eye to ETA activities, as they had done before, and extradited ETA militants back to Spain for prosecution. Basic militant operations in ETA was then passed into the hands of ETA youth groups, which instigated attacks in urban settings using guerilla tactics.

ETA terrorists were arrested and imprisoned in Spain. Some of the attacks subsided, and ETA again attempted to negotiate. Because of the gravity of the situation, the Spanish government refused to negotiate and considered them a criminal organization.

The Murder of Miguel Ángel Blanco

In 1997, a young Basque politician and councilor named Miguel Ángel Blanco was kidnapped by ETA. They indicated he would be released if ETA prisoners held in Spain were transferred to Basque prisons. The government refused, and Blanco was shot, after which he was dragged into the streets of San Sebastián. Blanco died in the hospital the next day on July 13th. Blanco was only twenty-five years old, and he was heralded as a hero to the cause of the People's Party, whose platform promotes democracy. His funeral was elaborate and very public. Not only was the government furious, but even some members of ETA and other militant organizations spoke out about the murder, condemning it. The Basque flag, called the ikurrina, was carried by the funeral train.

Memorial to Miguel Ángel Blanco

ETA held off their terror attacks during the 1998 Basque elections. The Basque Nationalists and the recently formed Euskal Herritarrok candidates won many seats, mostly due to the fact that the terrorist attacks had been suspended.

ETA Resumes Attacks

ETA resumed its terrorist attacks in 2000 (it should be noted ETA youth groups continued to promote the cause of nationalism throughout the years). In 2000, there were nearly fifty attacks on military, police, officials, politicians, journalists, and Basque companies. Not all the attacks took place in the Basque Country; many took place in Spain itself, especially Madrid. There were almost as many attacks the following year. These often did not involve gunfire, but many included bombs.

In 2002, Spain passed a law banning any organization that either directly or indirectly condoned violence as a means of forwarding its agenda. Newspapers that fostered violence were also banned.

Perhaps a Savior on the Rise

In 2004, José Luis Rodríguez Zapatero was elected as the new president of Spain. He held peace talks with ETA and the Basque and Spanish governments. A ceasefire was declared, but it was quickly broken by ETA, and attacks resumed all around Spain. In less than a year, four of their main leaders were arrested and imprisoned. By 2008, the government then banned some political parties they felt promoted or instigated violence, such as the Basque Nationalist Action, the youth groups, the Abertzale leftists, the Communist Party of the Basque Homelands, and others.

In 2011, the issue was brought to the international stage when citizens' groups from the Basque Country organized a meeting with leaders of other nations, including those who had dealt with similar issues. Among the attendees was Kofi Annan of the United Nations; Gro Harlem

Brundtland, former Prime Minister of Norway; Bertie Ahearn, former Prime Minister of Ireland; Pierre Joxe, former interior minister of France; Gerry Adams, President of Sinn Féin; and Johnathan Powell, former Chief of Staff in England. Gerry Adams, for one, advocated that the Spanish government open a dialogue with ETA rather than refusing to talk to them. Bertie Ahearn of Ireland received a peace award in the Basque Country for his role in the conference. After the efforts of this international group, ETA declared "definitive cessation of its armed activity."

France then contacted Spain and apprised them of the fact that these activities hadn't ceased in the French Basque Country. There were still a number of weapons and ammunition caches on the French side of the border. The French hired some non-governmental groups to go into the Nationalists' dens and storage facilities. ETA members in France gave them the locations of their stashes, which were then confiscated by French and Spanish authorities.

As popular pressure against ETA increased and financial support waned, membership fell off dramatically. Most Basques who favored secession wanted to approach the issue with non-violence.

Finally, on May 3rd, 2018, ETA declared an end to their terrorism and put it in writing. President Luis Zapatero said this was "a victory for democracy, law and reason."

Chapter 11 – The Basque Country Today

The Northern Basque Country is physically located in France, and the Southern Basque Country is within the geographic borders of Spain. The term they use for their country is *Euskal Herria*, which simply means the "Basque Country" in their native tongue of *Euskara*.

The French Basque Country doesn't have its own individual administration. It is incorporated into France as the Pyrénées-Atlantique. The French Basques are currently calling for a separate administration and even use the term "Département du Pays Basque."

French Basque seashore

Martin Stiburek, CC BY-SA 4.0 <https://creativecommons.org/licenses/by-sa/4.0>, via Wikimedia Commons https://commons.wikimedia.org/wiki/File:San_Sebasti%C3%A1n_7472.JPG

The Southern Basque Country consists of the Basque Autonomous Community and the Chartered Community of Navarre. By virtue of the Spanish Constitution of 1978, Navarre's populace didn't elect to become an autonomous community; instead, the people of Navarre still operate via the *fueros*, or charters of the past. The mainstream political party, the Navarrese People's Union, which is conservative, had preferred that arrangement, as they feared that many of the Leftists in Navarre would control too much power. For the justification of this move, the Navarrese relied upon what is called consuetudinary law, which is essentially a law that evolved through customary practice. A king was elected, along with a justice department. Most laws were based on older laws or customs.

Spanish Basque seashore

In Spain, the Statute of Basque Autonomy, also called the Statute of Gernika, was passed in 1979. It allows the provinces of Álava (Araba-Álava), Biscay, and Gipuzkoa to operate with their own government. It is similar to the states of America, though they are not subject to all federal laws. Each autonomous community has its own executive, legislative, and judicial system.

Basque Parliament and Government

The main body of the Basque Autonomous Community is located in the city of Vitoria-Gasteiz, just south of the city of Bilbao, in Álava, Spain. It is the umbrella of the local governing bodies.

The head administrator, called the *lehendakari*, is elected by the Basque Parliament. He is a member of a political party and has the most power in the Basque Autonomous Community. Instead of an individual head, a community might choose to have a coalition government composed of people representing various political parties.

The Basque Parliament consists of elective positions. The members legislate and monitor the actions and activities of the main government. Parliamentary duties include establishing and approving budgets. It is composed of seventy-five members, who serve for four years. Each territory has twenty-five representatives, regardless of population. These officials come from various political parties, but they must have a minimum of 5 percent of votes to qualify to run for office.

Departments are headed by appointed ministers. Below are some examples of the various departments.

Official Local Organization for the Historic Provinces

1. Provincial Administration

2. Juntas Generales ("General Councils")

There are fifty-one members of the Juntas Generales. They oversee a territory or district and are elected. They pass local regulations, including local budgets. They select the members of the Provincial Councils.

3. Provincial Councils

They are selected by the Juntas Generales. They appoint a team of deputies to perform various functions.

4. Town Councils

Council members are elective positions and are headed by a mayor. They provide transportation, fire department, sanitation, and the like. They charge local taxes for these services.

Public Resources and Administrative Departments

The Basque Country has all the services found in other countries. This includes:

Office of the President

Office of the Vice President

Department of Public Administration

Department of Finance

Department of Education

Department of Industry, Tourism, and Trade

Department of the Interior

Department of Housing and Social Affairs

Department of Culture

Department of Health

Department of Justice, Social Security, and Employment

Department of Transportation and Public Works

Department of the Environment

Department of Agriculture and Fishing

The current president of the Basque Country is Íñigo Urkullu. He hails from the Basque Nationalist Party. Ever since the protests and tragic terrorism felt as a result of ETA, the country has become very sensitive to political party matters. Currently, Andoni Ortuzar is the president of the Basque Nationalist Party. At the moment, the Nationalist Party is calling for more of a voice in issues within the Spanish Constitution that relate specifically to the Basque Country.

The president and vice president of the Basques have vital responsibilities in managing relations with the European Union. They also maintain close relations with Basques living abroad. The vice president's office also created the Basque Agency for Women. Their main focus is to ensure there are equal opportunities for women in Basque society. In fact, the Law on Equality between Men and Women was passed in 2005.

The Department of Finance and the Department of Public Administration oversee the budget and administer taxes, which includes public and foreign finances. The Department of Public Administration trains its personnel and all government employees working for public agencies.

The Department of Education guarantees free public education from infancy to the age of eighteen. School attendance is compulsory. Secondary education is also compulsory. Education beyond this is offered, which includes universities, polytechnic schools, and professional schools. Adult education courses are provided and feature the teaching of *Euskara* and Spanish.

The Department of Industry, Trade, and Tourism has web sites open to all Basques, including Basques living abroad. They have two important societies attached to it: the Association of Competitiveness, Science, and Technology, as well as the Basque Energy Board and the Society for the Promotion of Industry.

The Department of the Interior is responsible for traffic, the police department, and the police academy.

The Department of Housing provides government-sponsored housing for those in need, as well as providing related subsidies for them. This includes a division that helps with repairing and refurbishing living quarters. The Department of Social Affairs relates to the Office of Immigration. Laws regarding immigration are enforced and amended continually. Integration programs are presented to allow for easier assimilation into the Basque society. Immigration education services are also offered. This department provides programs for senior citizens, families, the disabled, drug addictions, and women.

The Department of Culture creates a calendar of public events open to all. Public theater, music, dance, and exhibitions are provided for the enjoyment and education of the public and tourists.

The Department of Health maintains the Basque hospitals, pharmacology centers, mental health facilities, and the like. It monitors drug prices for generic medications and provides information on the brands available.

The Department of Transportation and Public Works is in charge of railways, roads, airports, sanitation, seaports, and marinas.

The Department of the Environment manages land use and its impact on natural resources. Policies are in place that aid in the overall master plan for environmental protection. Future plans for land development go through this agency for approval and advice. Education programs are also offered.

The Department of Agriculture and Fishing deals with issues related to the use of lands for agriculture and fishing. An important factor is the proper protection of the environment and the avoidance of overexploitation of natural resources. Regulations for the proper raising of domestic wildlife are in place.

The Department of Justice, Social Security, and Employment oversees retirement benefits and unemployment. This includes job training if it is needed. It also provides for the training of public employees. There is an ancillary section that covers issues of job safety related to the workplace, accident prevention, and worker hygiene.

Local Practices

Humanitarian rights are enshrined in the local communities, especially the right not to be mistreated. Local responsibilities might be allocated by elections or even the drawing of lots to assume certain responsibilities.

The High Court of Justice

The court has thirteen members. Six are elected, and the other six are magistrates who have judicial powers pertinent to the offices they occupy. The last member is the president of the High Court of Justice. There are also presidents of the specific courts, namely the civil and criminal courts, the "contentious administration court," labor courts, and the magistrates of the provincial courts of Biscay, Álava, and Gipuzkoa.

The "contentious" court hears cases on appeals that deal with individual matters and the contended actions of administrators or administrations of governmental bodies. It is served by nine magistrates.

Labor courts hear cases related to the interests of employees, and they utilize tribunals to hear cases related to labor conflicts and bankruptcy. Ten magistrates serve in the labor courts.

Taxes

Tax agreements with Spain and the autonomous Basque regions are individually made. There are quotas that cover the provision of money for services provided by each Basque province that are not covered by Spain. For example, the individual provinces pay for road repairs, sanitation, local transportation, education, and the like. Spain provides the expenses for defense, foreign affairs, international representation, the running and maintenance of airports and seaports, and high-speed transportation for all its citizens, including the Basques.

Since 1981, the average quota for a Basque in an autonomous community is 6.24 percent of the national budget.

Each autonomous Basque community has its own personal income taxes, corporate taxes, inheritance taxes, and gift taxes. This money goes into the treasuries of the individual communities. Value-added taxes are charged by the communities on certain products, such as alcoholic beverages.

The Family Unit

Families in the Basque Country are composed much like the families of democratic cultures. Most consist of a heterosexual couple, who may or may not have children. This is true for about 44 percent of the population. There are also single parents living on their own, which represent about 20 percent of the population. Some live in family groups, like extended families.

Homosexuality isn't forbidden in Spain and the Basque Country. If a same-sex couple gets married in Spain, where it is recognized, the marriage is also recognized in the Basque Country.

As of 2003, domestic partnerships—two unmarried people living together—is rather common in the Basque Country. Unlike arrangements in other countries, these couples have the same rights and obligations as married couples. However, they do need to register as a couple in a domestic partnership. This even includes same-sex marriages, except in the case of the death of one of the partners. In that case, widower's pensions are not allowed. Regardless of sexual preference, all marriages permit adoptions, and they must pay taxes.

In 2005, the Gender Equality Act was passed. Emakunde is the institution attached to the office of the president that advises, coordinates, evaluates, and promotes gender equality for women. It works to ensure that gender equality is implemented in education, health, employment, culture, and social services.

Education

Education is provided free of charge. It is compulsory from ages six to sixteen. At the age of sixteen, students have the option to continue their education for two more years, provided they have satisfactory grades.

Students may then pursue academic studies through preparation training to enter college, or they can take professional courses to ready themselves for an occupation. Following the death of Francisco Franco, schools called *ikastolak* were created. Those schools are of four types: X, which teaches only in Spanish; A, which teaches in Spanish with Basque as a compulsory subject; B, which teaching is partly in Spanish and partly in Basque; and D, which education is taught only in Basque. It is interesting to note that 50 percent of the students elect to attend the all-Basque language schools.

There are four universities in the Basque Country: the public University of the Basque Country; the University of Deusto, a Jesuit-run university; the Opus Dei-run University of Navarre, a Catholic university; and the University of Mondragon, run by the Mondragon Corporation.

Business

Labor unions, called "class unions," aren't organized for each particular company. Instead, they represent all workers. Most are divided into geographical areas. ELA, which stands for *Eusko Langileen Alkartasuna* ("Basque Workers' Solidarity"), is nationalistic and supports the provinces in the Basque Country. CCOO is a huge labor union in Spain, and it oversees the Basque Country as well. CCOO stands for *Comisiones Obereras* ("Workers' Commissions"). There are also smaller unions representing different sectors of the country, such as education or health. Other unions represent the self-employed and farmers.

Many businesses are cooperatives, which are businesses that are run and owned by the workers. The Mondragon Corporation is an umbrella for 257 cooperative companies, which employ a little over 74,000 people. Not all of the workers live in the Basque Country. The beauty of the Mondragon Corporation is the fact that money is taken out of the general funds to rescue a member company that might be on the verge of bankruptcy.

The Basque business sector is virulent and above the general EU (European Union) average. Metalworks and steel are still their strongest industrial sectors, and they also make machine tools. Petrochemical products, aeronautics, and energy production are also strong.

Mondragon Corporation

The Mondragon Corporation is the largest cooperative corporation in the Basque Country. It was founded in 1941 by a priest named José María

Arizmendiarrieta, and its original purpose was to help the Basques after the Spanish Civil War. The country had been devastated by poverty, and it was in sore need of educated labor. Arizmendiarrieta built a college that trained its students to be skilled technicians, engineers, and other trained laborers.

The Mondragon Corporation employs humanistic principles of understanding and mutual cooperation in improving its member companies. One of its pivotal principles is self-sufficiency. Their objective is to create companies that do not need to be too dependent upon other industries for survival. In some ways, it is the antithesis of the kind of competition that pits one company against another. Mondragon has a unique approach toward business, as it doesn't place the accumulation of wealth as its sole overriding precept. Factors like safety and quality feature high on their set of priorities. They are, of course, interested in profit but not to its extreme. Workers contribute to the cooperative to the extent of their abilities.

Mondragon holds up the rights of the workers and minimizes the exploitation of labor in favor of profit. In addition, it avoids heavily paying the few corporate executives on top so the benefits can be spread around to the other workers.

The Basque industrial area is in the north, and it progressively gets more agricultural as one heads south.

Culture

The Basques love festivals. The Festival of San Fermín, also known as the Running of the Bulls, is known worldwide. It goes on for a week, and it includes more than just the running of the bulls. Parades feature giant puppets dressed in what is known as "Basque Red," one of the colors in their flag.

It originated in the 13th century when bulls were shipped into Pamplona by barges in order to be brought to the market. Young men were assigned to run alongside the bulls to lead them through the streets and into their corrals to be auctioned off. After a while, they made a sport of it. Bullfights are also a popular pastime in both Spain and the Basque Country.

July and August are the most popular months for festivals and fairs. These celebrations are quite imaginative. For the Virgen Blanca celebration, a doll named Celedón, so-called after Juan Celedonio de Anzola from Vitoria-Gasteiz in the province of Álava, descends on a wire from the belfry at the Church of San Miguel to a balcony over New Square. He carries an umbrella, like the character Mary Poppins. Once the doll arrives, a real person, who is supposed to be the embodiment of Celedón, appears on the street. He gives a brief speech, which is followed by parades, cooking contests, bullfights, and fireworks.

Sports

The Basques have a series of rural sports and competitions, such as wood-chopping, hole drilling, scything, bale tossing, cob-carrying, stone lifting, and even tug-of-war. Animal-related competitions like ram fighting, sheep shearing, and donkey racing also take place.

The idi probak is a competition requiring an ox, horse, or donkey to drag heavy stones across a distance.

Their main sporting events are called pelota, which consists of a variety of handball-inspired court games.

Jai Alai

The sport of jai alai originated in the Basque Country in the 14th century. The Basque term for it is *zesta punta*, which literally means "basket tip." It is a variation of pelota. The sport has spread to Spain, France, North and South America, the Philippines, and Cuba. There are

World Championship games held yearly. Jai alai is also one of the events in the Olympics.

The Tamborrada de San Sebastián Festival consists of parades and bands. It has a military flavor, as the drums are usually hand-crafted. They are based on designs from its original creator, an anonymous baker who started beating on barrels he was filling near San Vincente Church in 1720. The Basque people are very creative, and they find pleasure by making work seem less of a chore.

In the city of Bilboa, the people celebrate the Assumption of Our Lady in what is called Aste Nagusia, or "Great Week." Its central event is a circus, and there are traditional dancing performances. It originated during the dictatorship of Francisco Franco. Dancers, or *danzarias*, wear white with red berets when they perform for the people in Bayonne in the French Basque Country during their annual fair.

Another popular event is a non-competitive sponsored auto race through a complex course laid out in the foothills of the Pyrenees. Proceeds go to a general fund to teach and preserve *Euskara*, the unique language of the Basques.

Basque Cuisine

The cuisine of the Basques differs from one part of the country to the other. It shows a mixture of what the sea offers, as well as meat dishes featuring lamb and spices, such as Espelette pepper.

Fish, such as salted cod, tuna, and other seafood, dominate the coastal regions. A favorite dish is marmitako or "tuna pot." The Basques use albacore (longfin) tuna to create this meal. Kokotxa is a fish stew made from the cheeks of a fatty fish, like hake or cod. It is usually served with a white sauce that is made green due to its heavy parsley content. Elvers, or small eels, are also popular. Maja Squinado is a spiny crab with very long legs, and the Basques stuff and bake the crabs in their own shells. It is a common dish in the Bay of Biscay area. Txipirones, or small squids, are also quite common in those waters and can be eaten with their ink. Piperade is a soup made from an assortment of vegetables, mostly tomatoes. It is similar in taste to ratatouille. One more popular item is talo, which is a corn-like tortilla that can be used as a sandwich wrap. The Basques tend to use olive oil rather than vegetable oil in cooking since it is of a higher quality.

Many Basque people are genetically lactose-intolerant. However, many can tolerate sheep milk. Hence, they have cheese products such as Roncal or Ossau-Iraty, which is cheese made from ewe's milk. Idiazabal is a spreadable cheese made from sheep's milk. The lactose in this product is generally washed out when the whey is discarded.

The inland areas eat a lot of cured meats, such as ham and lamb sausage. Vegetables and legumes are plentiful in the fertile Ebro Valley. Txakoli is a popular light white or sparkling green wine that is low in alcoholic content and has a short shelf life. It originated in the Álava province, but there is a light rosé variety in Cantabria.

Apple cider is a popular alcoholic beverage in the Basque Country. Cider houses are called sidrerías in the Basque language. They also offer cod omelets and other light snacks. Red and rosé wines are produced in the Spanish vineyards of the province of Rioja. The city of Getaria in the Basque province of Gipuzkoa produces white wines.

The Basque Diaspora

Throughout the years, many Basques have left the Basque Country and settled in other parts of the world. Outside of France and Spain, the highest number of Basques have resettled in Columbia, Chile, and Argentina. There are also communities in Venezuela, Mexico, Peru, Cuba, Uruguay, Russia, other parts of Asia, Canada, the United States, and Saint Pierre and Miquelon. Saint Pierre and Miquelon is a group of

French-owned islands in the northwestern Atlantic Ocean near Canada. The Basque communities have been there for many years and are mostly the descendants of Basque fishermen. The Basque flag is flown there, and it is the unofficial flag for these islands.

Conclusion

The history of the Basques is rather convoluted, as these proud people have been manipulated by much larger nations throughout the ages. Today, the Basques number about three million, and they have fought the good fight to preserve their language and culture from unjustifiable raids from others.

Throughout time, many civilizations who prized assimilation popped up, wanting to make the Basques more like them. Between 1936 and 1975, Francisco Franco, the dictator of Spain, forbade the Basques to speak their own native language. This was a common theme in history. Way back in 196 BCE, the ancient Romans tried to Romanize the Basques. Fortunately, neither Rome nor Franco was successful.

When the various territories of the Basque people were conquered by one foreign nation after another, no attention was paid to keeping their respective territories intact. Dividing up the Basque territories seemed to become an international game. What is more astonishing is the fact that these conquered territories were often renamed. Throughout the years, there was little effort spent on spelling the names of their people or their provinces in a consistent manner.

So, it is no wonder the Basque people of today have exerted a great deal of effort to preserve their language. In fact, long-term visitors have said they found it a valuable asset to learn *Euskara*, as they are awarded more respect for having done so.

It is amazing to note that these people, whose ancestry dates back to Paleolithic times, haven't lost much of the purity of their ethnicity. Researchers, ethnologists, and even medical clinicians have engaged in modern-day studies about these people. The Basques have been a subject of research all the way down to the level of their unique DNA.

The Basques are clever and intelligent. They have been practical since ancient times, having learned early on that one can earn money by being a mercenary in all the wars that peppered history. They also knew how to utilize their resources, and they were perhaps the most skilled whale hunters on the continent in the 15th century. It was the Basques who mined gold and silver for the Roman currency. The numismatists of today still sell Basque coins from ancient times.

The most prominent and laudable characteristic of the Basques is the fact that they work together. The comradery they have for each other is their greatest survival skill, and it has only grown throughout the centuries. Even their business community thrives on cooperation, rather than cut-throat competition. This is perhaps the key to their survival through the many wars fought around or even on their land.

Here's another book by Captivating History that you might like

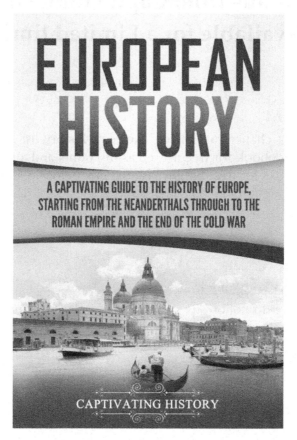

Free Bonus from Captivating History (Available for a Limited time)

Hi History Lovers!

Now you have a chance to join our exclusive history list so you can get your first history ebook for free as well as discounts and a potential to get more history books for free! Simply visit the link below to join.

Captivatinghistory.com/ebook

Also, make sure to follow us on Facebook, Twitter and Youtube by searching for Captivating History.

Bibliography

"Ancient DNA: Neanderthal" Retrieved from:

https://australian.museum/learn/science/human-evolution/homo-heidelbergensis/#:~:text=Homo%20heidelbergensis%20began%20to%20develop,our%20own%20species%2C%20Homo%20sapiens.

Barton, S. (2009). A History of Spain. Red Globe Press.

"Basque History of the World" Retrieved from: https://erenow.net/common/the-basque-history-of-the-world/3.php.

Braudel, F. (1976). The Mediterranean and the Mediterranean World in the Age of Philip II (2 vols.) University of California Press.

Carballo, D. M. (2020). Collision of Worlds. Oxford University Press.

Cabrera, M. A. (2005). "Developments in Contemporary Spanish Historiography: From Social History to the New Cultural History," Journal of Modern History.

Carr, R. (1982). Spain, 1808-1975 (2nd ed.). Oxford University Press.

Conrada, J. W. (1977). A Bibliographical Guide to Spanish Diplomacy 1460-1977. Greenwood Press.

Linehan, P. (1993). History and Historians of Medieval Spain. Oxford University Press.

Elliott, J. H. (1963). Imperial Spain: 1469-1716. Penguin Press.

Hertzberger, D. K. (1995). Narrating the Past: Fiction and Historiography in Postwar Spain. Duke University Press.

"Homo Heidelbergensis" Retrieved from: https://australian.museum/learn/science/human-evolution/homo-heidelbergensis/#:~:text=Homo%20heidelbergensis%20began%20to%20develop,our%20own%20species%2C%20Homo%20sapiens.

"Iron Age Iberians" Retrieved from: https://geology.com/rocks/iron-ore.shtml#:~:text=Nearly%20all%20of%20Earth%27s%20major,releasing%20oxygen%20into%20the%20waters.

Kamen, H. (2005). Spain: A Society of Conflict. Pearson Longmen.

Kennedy, H. (1996). Muslim Spain and Portugal: A Political History of al-Andalus (1st ed.). Routledge.

Lane-Poole, S. (2011). The Moors in Spain. Kindle.

"Livia: Spanish Wars" Retrieved from: https://www.livius.org/sources/content/appian/appian-the-spanish-wars/appian-the-spanish-wars-12/#60.

"New Evidence: Neanderthal Hybrid" Retrieved from : https://archaeologynewsnetwork.blogspot.com/2017/10/new-excavations-confirm-spains-el-pendo.html#M2UmAL0p8YGlcJfX.97.

Phillips, W. D., Jr. and Carla R. Phillips (2010). A Concise History of Spain. Cambridge University Press.

"Studies of Spain" Retrieved from: http://countrystudies.us/spain/4.htm.

Treaty of Lutatius" Retrieved from: https://en.wikipedia.org/wiki/Treaty_of_Lutatius.

"Ancient DNA Cracks Puzzle on Basque Origins" Retrieved from https://www.bbc.com/news/science-environment-34175224

"Basque Country: A Land of Myths and Legends"
https://www.bizkaiatalent.eus/en/pais-vasco-te-espera/senas-de-identidad/vasco-tierra-leyendas/

"Basque Mythology, Ancestral Religion, Spirituality and Modern Religion" Retrieved from

https://aaconventionbiarritz.com/2019/08/29/basque-mythology-ancestral-religion-spirituality-and-modern-religions/

"The Basque Problem" Retrieved from https://erenow.net/common/the-basque-history-of-the-world/3.php

"The Basque Paradigm" Maternal Evidence of a Maternal Continuity in the Franco-Cantabrian

Region since Neolithic Times" Retrieved from

https://www.ncbi.nlm.nih.gov/pmc/articles/PMC3309182/

"A Brief History of the Pamplona Citadel and City Walls" Retrieved from

https://theculturetrip.com/europe/spain/articles/a-brief-history-of-the-pamplona-citadel-and-city-walls/

Cabarello, D. "Parity in Government: Gender Equality within the Basque Government" Retrieved

from https://blogs.shu.edu/basqueresearch/2015/12/01/parity-in-parliament-gender-equality-within-the-basque-government/

Collins, Roger, Gillingham, J. (ed.) (1984) "The Basques in Aquitaine and Navarre: Problems of Frontier Government". War and Society in the Middle Ages: Essays in Honor of J. O. Prestwich.

Boydell Press

"History of Basque II" Retrieved from
http://www.kondaira.net/eng/Euskara2.html

"History of the Basque People" Retrieved from
https://thereaderwiki.com/en/History_of_the_Basque_people

"History of the Basque Wars" Retrieved from
http://forwhattheywereweare.blogspot.com/2011/10/history-of-basque-wars-i.html

"The History of Navarre" Retrieved from

http://www.bbc.co.uk/history/british/middle_ages/hundred_years_war_01.shtml

"The Hundred Years War" Retrieved from

http://www.bbc.co.uk/history/british/middle_ages/hundred_years_war_01.shtml

Watson, C. (2003) Modern Basque History: Eighteenth Century to the Present University of Nevada, Center for Basque Studies

Made in United States
Orlando, FL
30 November 2024

54687371R00153